Studies in English Transformational Grammar

Studies in English Transformational Grammar

By Sven Jacobson

Stockholm 1971

Printed with the aid of a grant from
Statens humanistiska forskningsråd

OC00203426

Printed in Sweden by

Almqvist & Wiksells Boktryckeri AB, Uppsala 1971

Contents

Acknowledgements

On the completion of this volume, which is based on seven years' work in English transformational grammar, my thanks are due to Professors M. T. Löfvenberg and Alarik Rynell for including it in the series *Stockholm Studies in English*. I also thank the latter for reading my whole manuscript and giving me many valuable comments.

To the following linguists, whose friendship I greatly appreciate, I owe a great debt of gratitude for penetrating criticisms and valuable advice on special papers in this volume:

Professors Sidney Greenbaum and Alvar Ellegård (an earlier and slightly longer version of paper no. 4),

Professors Paul Kiparsky and Jan Svartvik (the original version underlying paper no. 5 and parts of paper no. 6),

Professor James McCawley (paper no. 7), and

Docent Östen Dahl (paper no. 8).

My thanks are further due to:

Professors Noam Chomsky and Jerrold Katz for granting me an interview at their research department in the Center for Cognitive Studies, Harvard University, in the summer of 1965, when I had the opportunity of discussing with them some points of transformational grammar which specially intrigued me,

Professors George and Robin Lakoff, and Professor John Robert Ross, for sending me some of their books and papers, and

Professor Sven Öhman for arranging and inviting me to attend the First Scandinavian Summer School of Linguistics in 1969 with such eminent lecturers as James McCawley, John Robert Ross, and Paul Kiparsky, who in two weeks taught me more about present-day linguistics than several months of study on my own.

Among colleagues and friends who have helped me in various ways and with whom I have enjoyed lengthy discussions on linguistic problems I would like to express my gratitude especially to Professor Johannes Söderlind, Docents Lars-Gunnar Hallander and Mats Rydén, Dr. Inger Ruin, Dr. Ferenc Kiefer, and Fil. lic. Karin Aijmer.

7

Finally I want to thank my room-mate at the English Department, Docent Sverker Brorström, and my wife and children for cheering me up when I got too entangled in my phrase-markers, like a fly in a cobweb.

Stockholm, November 1970

Sven Jacobson
The English Department
Stockholm University

Introduction

The eight papers included in this volume deal with various central aspects of transformational grammar, such as sentence generation, functional relations, explanatory power, and the general organization of the grammar, but some special fields are also treated, e.g. adverbials, auxiliaries, and tense.

Cutting across this horizontal description of different aspects of grammar is a vertical axis of time: the papers were composed during a period of seven years, 1964–1970, and thus reflect different stages in the historical development of transformational grammar.

All the papers have been printed in the original form in which they appeared in the years of composition indicated in the Table of Contents.[1] Only certain minor alterations, which do not affect the ideas laid down, have been made in some of the papers. For example, titles have had to be given to papers which were originally intended as chapters or sections of larger works. In this connection I wish to point out that the papers, as they appear here, do not in all details represent my views at the present moment. I willingly admit that I have had to revise many of my earlier ideas in the light of the continuing evolution of transformational grammar. I even desire the papers to mirror how my views have changed, for I regard a "revisionary" attitude as necessary for one doing research in present-day linguistics: an opposite attitude would only bear evidence of stagnation. Even Noam Chomsky himself does not adhere today to all the details of his famous work *Syntactic Structures*, although he no doubt still agrees with the essential message that this book propagated in 1957, when it was first published. Alvar Ellegård, in an article in *Dagens Nyheter* (25 February 1965) has characterized this publication as the beginning of a great revolution in linguistics. It seems, however, as if this revolution is going to take a very long time, before final victory in the form of a complete transformational-generative description of language is attained, if it is ever attained, for with every bit of ground gained new areas of linguistic wilderness loom ahead, full of paradoxes and baffling facts. Perhaps a more down-to-earth characterization of present-day linguistics would be to compare it with a game of constant trial and error.

---

[1] This is the reason why in some papers British spelling is used, in others American.

An attempt to apply Chomsky's ideas, as they were laid down in *Syntactic Structures*, to one special area of grammar was made in 1960 by Robert Lees, who in his book *The Grammar of English Nominalizations* introduced a great number of detailed rules for phrase-structure, transformations, and morphophonemics. In 1964 there appeared four important books, which together give a good indication of the development of the theory so far: Noam Chomsky, *Current Issues in Linguistic Theory*, Emmon Bach, *An Introduction to Transformational Grammars*, Jerrold Katz and Paul Postal, *An Integrated Theory of Linguistic Descriptions*, and Paul Postal, *Constituent Structure*. In his book Chomsky discusses, amongst other things, three different levels of success for linguistic descriptions, viz. explanatory, descriptive, and observational adequacy, and shows that only a theory which like transformational grammar uses a rigorously applied technique can attain the first level. Bach tries to give a simple step-by-step presentation of the main concepts and techniques of transformational grammar, and the purpose of Katz and Postal is to incorporate the grammatical and semantic descriptions of language into one integrated description. It is in their book that the well-known thesis that transformations do not change the meaning of deep structures is first established. Postal, finally, considers eight major formulations of American descriptive grammar and claims that they are essentially phrase-structure grammars and thus cannot be regarded as reasonable alternatives of transformational grammar.

In paper no. 1, which I wrote that year, I tried to summarize the main ideas about sentence generation that had been put forth so far, and I introduced in the section on functional relations the two concepts of sentence-operators and phrase-operators and illustrated their difference by a number of examples, especially such as involved various types of adverbials. The term "operate" was actually borrowed from British linguistics, where it is usual to say, for example, that the verbal group operates at a place called V in the clause. The paper ends by making the claim that an adverb like *especially* can in certain contexts have three functions simultaneously. Two years later I enlarged upon this idea in an article entitled "The Problem of Describing Syntactic Complexity" (Jacobson 1968a: 119–25).

In the earlier part of the next year, 1965, I began to question the current idea of generating adverbials by means of phrase-structure rules and began investigations to substantiate the opposite approach that all adverbials, except adverbial particles, are generated by transformational rules, called adverbializations. This idea is propounded in paper no. 2.

In the summer of 1965 came the publication of Noam Chomsky, *Aspects of the Theory of Syntax*, which I reviewed in the December 1966 issue of *Linguistics*. The time had now come for Chomsky, after several years of vindicating the fundamental tenets of his theory, to revise, extend, and deepen many of his earlier formulations.

In the same year H. A. Gleason, Jr., published his book *Linguistics and English Grammar*, in which he devotes a great deal of space to a discussion of three types of generative grammar, each based on some earlier technique of grammatical description. Paper no. 3 ends with a reference to this book but is mainly devoted to some grammatical discussions, which are meant to illustrate Chomsky's claim that transformational grammar has great explanatory power. One passage of the original paper has here been omitted, since it has already appeared in print as pages 125–27 of my review of Mats Rydén, *Relative Constructions in Early Sixteenth Century English* in the November 1968 issue of *Linguistics*. Later I returned to the subject of explanatory power in a paper entitled "Transformational Grammar and Linguistic Intuition" (Jacobson 1967).

In 1966 Owen Thomas published his pedagogical work *Transformational Grammar and the Teacher of English*, which was the first popular survey of transformational grammar after the major revision in 1965. One thing that intrigued me in this book was a statement made on p. 163 that "in the opinion of the author the preverbs", i.e. "such adverbs as *almost, always, ever, seldom, rarely*" are "the least understood subclass of adverbs". I decided to investigate this subclass and in 1967–68 wrote a working paper, which was circulated in mimeographed form in the earlier half of 1968 under the title *The Placement of Preverbs in American English*, Introduction and Chapter I, "The Classification of Preverbs".[2] In the version printed here as paper no. 4 certain formal changes necessitated by turning chapter I into an independent paper have been made. For example, references to my quantitative investigation have been deleted and only the first part of section 4 has been included. Moreover, some minor errors have been corrected and the clumsy term "attention-directer" has been replaced by "focalizer".

With the rapid development of transformational grammar the approach used in this survey of preverbs became outdated before I had time to write the rest of the book. This applies in particular to the phrase-structure rules and the phrase-markers based on them. This outdating was mainly due to the development of a new theory concerning the generation of auxiliaries.

---

[2] One of those who received a copy was Sidney Greenbaum, who mentions it in his book *Studies in English Adverbial Usage*, pp. 234 and 252.

The use of the constituent Aux as a deep structure category was now refuted and different ideas about its replacement were propounded. I realized that the criticism against the phrase-structure generation of auxiliaries was justified, but decided to make my own investigation of how they might be derived by transformational rules. The result was paper no. 5 (1968), which in footnote 4 gives a survey of arguments that were used in the debate on the Aux constituent. Admittedly, the transformational rules given in this paper are far from easy to read, but as far as comprehensibility is concerned, I am sure they can well stand comparison with the chapters entitled "Aspect— Perfect and Progressive", "The Auxiliary", and "Agreement" in the *English Transformational Grammar* by Roderick Jacobs and Peter Rosenbaum, which came out in the same year. This grammar represents the peak of the feature period in transformational grammar. Today the new approach of Generative Semantics has given alternative ways of representing what was earlier achieved by means of features. See paper no. 7 (especially section 2b).

Paper no. 5 was presented at the postgraduate English seminar of Gothenburg University in November 1968 in connection with a guest lecture which Jan Svartvik had invited me to deliver. It differs from the version distributed at the seminar meeting in that the section, rule, and figure numbering has been changed owing to the omission of irrelevant sections. Moreover, certain minor amendments resulting from the discussion after my lecture have been made.

Among the irrelevant sections omitted was an earlier version of paper no. 6. This version was revised in the earlier half of 1969 and is here printed essentially in the form I then gave it. Editing it as a paper in 1970 required, however, a certain degree of reorganization, and some additions and omissions were made. In paper no. 4 I had, under the influence of Chomsky's lexicalist position (Chomsky 1967), somewhat modified my original idea that all adverbials are to be derived transformationally, but I now returned to it by including no phrase-structure rules with the category Adv, only a feature [+adv], which had the object of triggering adverbialization transformations.

A paper which I composed about the same time as paper no. 6 and which deals with a similar theme has recently been published in *Moderna Språk* 1970, no. 2, under the title "An Example of the Positioning of Concurrent Adverbs".[3]

In the summer of 1969 I attended the First Scandinavian Summer School

---

[3] The reference in footnote 11 of this paper should be to paper no. 6 in this volume instead of to Jacobson (in preparation).

of Linguistics, where John Ross lectured on syntax, James McCawley on semantics, and Paul Kiparsky on phonology. Here I was given an excellent introduction to the theory of generative semantics, and on the basis of the lectures by Ross and McCawley and the papers that were distributed to us for individual study I wrote paper no. 7 (1970). It is an attempt to explain the present situation with two rival factions within the transformational school. On the one side are those who are adherents of Chomsky's standard theory, either in its original form as laid down in *Aspects of the Theory of Syntax* or in a form including its lexicalist and interpretivist modifications, and on the other those who embrace the emergent theory of generative semantics or some related theory such as Charles Fillmore's case grammar (Fillmore 1968). The battle that is now being waged with fierce attacks from both sides can be watched, for example, in the May 1970 issue of *Foundations of Language* in such articles as "On the Alleged Boundary between Syntax and Semantics" by Frederick Newmeyer and "Interpretative Semantics vs. Generative Semantics" by Jerrold Katz. At least one attempt has, however, been made to bridge the gap between the two factions. It is *The Study of Syntax* by Terence Langendoen, who has based the earlier part of his book mainly on Chomsky's standard theory, whereas the latter part is based on ideas from generative semantics and Fillmore's case grammar.

Paper no. 8 is a practical demonstration of how the methods of generative semantics can be used in an examination of a particular field of grammar, in this case the two pairs of "janus" categories logical tense/deep tense and formal tense/surface tense. My final conclusion is that the relationship between these two pairs can be explained by a fifth category, called intermediate tense.

1. Sentence Generation and Functional Relations in Transformational Grammar

1. Sentence Generation

Sentence generation in transformational grammar proceeds roughly along the following lines. The first step is to use the rule

(Rule 1) $S \rightarrow NP + VP$

i.e. a sentence[1] is a binary structure consisting of a noun phrase and a verb phrase.[2] By further rules these phrases in their turn may be rewritten into other phrases and finally into formatives (i.e. minimal syntactically functioning elements such as words or morphemes), class markers,[3] and juncture, sentence-stress and intonation markers.[4] By this rewriting procedure the sentence is mechanically assigned a structural description which can be illustrated by a phrase-marker (P-marker) in the form of a labelled tree (fig. 1). The rewrite rules are usually called phrase-structure (PS) rules,[5] and they generate a C-terminal string.[6] This string of formatives constitutes the terminal vocabulary, while the initial symbol (S) and the various phrase symbols (NP, VP, etc.) constitute the non-terminal vocabulary.[7]

---

[1] For a discussion of the term 'sentence' in transformational grammar, see Gleason 1961, p. 190.

[2] On the use of binary structures see, for instance, Chomsky 1961, p. 23; Gleason 1961, pp. 180–81 and 192; Postal 1964, p. 87, fn. 60.

[3] Cf. Chomsky 1964a, pp. 915 and 944 (= Chomsky 1964b, pp. 9 and 65–66).

[4] Cf. Stockwell 1960. These prosodic elements are often left unmarked.

[5] Another common term is 'constituent structure rules'. The abbreviation then used, CS, is however slightly ambiguous as it is also employed in the sense 'context-sensitive'. Cf. Bach 1964, p. 35.

[6] C stands for 'constituent'. Cf. Chomsky 1964a, p. 917 (= 1964b, p. 12).

[7] Cf. Chomsky 1959, p. 140.

14

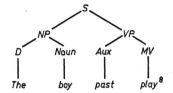

Fig. 1. P-marker of the sentence *The boy played*. D = determiner, Aux = auxiliary (Chomsky 1957, p. 39), MV = main verb.

On the derivational path[9] from an element in the terminal string to the node labelled S there is often a node with a phrase label even in cases where this latter node has no branching lines leading to different words (see, for instance, the word *John* in fig. 2b).[10]

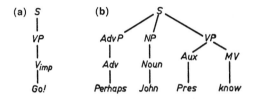

Fig. 2. Derived P-markers showing deletion of NP (*a*) and addition of AdvP (*b*). AdvP = adverb phrase.

If we want a string generated by PS-rules to contain less than NP + VP, for instance if we want an imperative sentence with only the verb phrase expressed, we have to use a deletion transformation.[11] Similarly, if we want to introduce a new branch, we have to use an addition transformation. Special transformational rules (T-rules), which can apply to singular, i.e. one-string, or generalized, i.e. two-string, transformations, are used in these cases.[12]

---

[8] This is the abstract C-terminal string underlying the real sentence *The boy played*. C-terminal strings usually underlie simple declarative active sentences. Cf. Chomsky 1957, p. 80, and 1961, p. 17.

[9] See Bach 1964, p. 72.

[10] Cf. Bach 1964, p. 79, the second diagram. Just as in traditional grammar we can say that a sentence consists of one or more words, so in transformational grammar a phrase can be rewritten into one or more formatives. Halliday uses terms in a similar manner when setting up his hierarchy of units: "The relation among the units, then, is that, going from top (largest) to bottom (smallest), each 'consists of' one, or of more than one, of the unit next below (next smaller)" (1961, p. 251).

[11] Cf. Gleason 1961, pp. 180–81.

[12] See Bach 1964, pp. 59–82.

When a generalized transformation is taking place, a constituent sentence (or string) may be embedded in a matrix sentence, or several strings may be conjoined.[13] P-markers on which transformations have been performed are called derived P-markers and the resultant strings are T-terminal strings.[14] Every such string includes in its derivational history a set of P-markers consisting of one, or in the case of generalized transformations two or more, underlying P-markers (i.e. P-markers mapping C-terminal strings) + one or more derived P-markers. The last one of a series of P-markers is called the final derived P-marker. The assignment of *sets* of P-markers to strings is perhaps the greatest difference between transformational grammar and other contemporary models of syntactic description.[15]

The PS-rules and T-rules so far discussed form the syntactic component of a transformational grammar. The terminal strings generated by this component are subject to the rules of two more components, dealing, respectively, with the phonological and the semantic aspects of language.

By means of a transformational cycle, preceded and followed by rewrite rules, the phonological component generates underlying abstract phonemes[16] and determines on the basis of these the phonetic form of a sentence.[17] The syntactic structure involved is only surface structure, i.e. that indicated by the final derived P-marker which maps the T-terminal string. The semantic component, on the other hand, operates with deep structure in that it gives a semantic interpretation of a sentence on the basis of the significant functions and relations that are expressed by underlying P-markers.[18]

The phonological component does not need to involve deep structure, as the phones of such a string as *The shooting of the soldiers* will be the same irrespective of whether it occurs in the first or the second of the following sentences:

The shooting of the soldiers took place at dawn and they were immediately buried.

The shooting of the soldiers was indiscriminate and many civilians were killed.

The semantic interpretation of the string, on the other hand, is based on

---

[13] Cf. Bach 1964, pp. 67 and 75.

[14] Cf. Chomsky 1964a, p. 917 (= 1964b, p. 13). Fillmore, in an article where he discusses the "traffic rules" between various transformations, speaks of pre-sentences instead of T-terminal strings (1963, p. 209).

[15] Cf. Postal 1964, pp. 51, 68, and 73.

[16] Phonemes are abstract in the sense that no one has ever uttered a phoneme. (Only phones are uttered.)

[17] Cf. Chomsky 1964a, pp. 917–18 (= 1964b, p. 13).

[18] Cf. Chomsky 1964b, pp. 10, 14, and 65.

the whole sentence context and is intimately connected with the string's transformational history, which includes either an underlying P-marker mapping *X shot the soldiers* or one mapping *The soldiers were shooting*. The semantic component, then, gives rules which account for the interaction between meaning and syntactic structure. Also, it has the purpose of accounting for semantic relations between morphemes, so that given a sentence such as *The bill is large*, which can have only one syntactic description, we know whether *bill* means, for instance, a tailor's bill or a bird's bill.[19]

The difference between the deep structure basis of the semantic component and the surface structure basis of the phonological component may be illustrated thus:

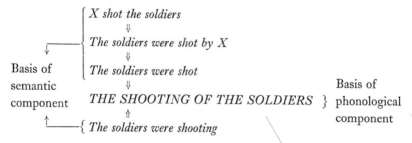

2. Functional Relations

As Rule 1 and figs. 1 and 2 show, formulas and P-markers in transformational grammar do not include such functional terms as 'subject', 'predicate', or 'object'.[20] One reason is that functional relationships are considered to be sufficiently expressed by the various subconfigurations within a P-marker.[21] Thus if NP and VP branch out direct from S, as in fig. 1, they must be in a subject–predicate relation. Sometimes subscripts are used which refer nodal class markers to particular subgroups. For example, the object relation in (*We*) *use miles* (*not kilometres*) can be distinguished from the adverbial modifier relation in (*We*) *walk miles* by indicating whether the verb is transitive (V_t) or intransitive (V_i), as in fig. 3.

---

[19] Cf. Katz and Fodor 1963, pp. 174 and 183.
[20] This is one important difference between transformational grammar and tagmemics, where both slot (= function) and filler (= class) are denoted. Instead of, for instance, NP + VP tagmemicists write $S^N + P^V$ (Pike) or S : N + P : V (Elson and Pickett), which means "subject slot filled by noun + predicate slot filled by verb".
[21] Cf. Chomsky 1964*b*, p. 61, and Postal 1964, pp. 37–38.

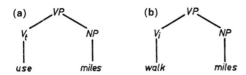

Fig. 3. Object relation (*a*) and adverbial modifier relation (*b*).

Another important functional distinction that can be made on the basis of P-markers is that between *sentence-operators* and various *phrase-operators*.

An element may be said to be sentence-operating, when on the derivational path from its place in the P-marker to the node labelled S there is no intervening branching node. In all other cases elements are phrase-operating. Fig. 4 shows how a phrase-operating adverbial particle can be turned by positional change into a sentence-operator.

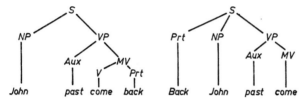

Fig. 4. P-markers of *John came back* and *Back John came.* MV = main verb, V = verb, Prt = particle (cf. Bach 1964, pp. 79–80).

Just as in ordinary sentences so in embedded sentences, elements can be either sentence- or phrase-operators depending on the nodes to which they are traceable. Thus *perhaps* is a sentence-operator in fig. 5, where it is traceable with no intervening branching node to S, but a phrase-operator in fig. 6 where it is traceable to S only via the branching node AdvP.

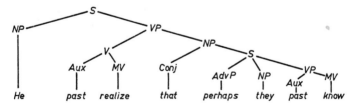

Fig. 5. P-marker of *He realized that perhaps they knew.* The element *that perhaps they past know* is classified as NP, because in the generalized transformation embedding one sentence in the other it has been substituted for the NP *it* in the matrix sentence (for a detailed description of generalized substitution transformation, see Dallaire 1963, pp. 28–33).

18

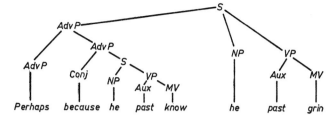

Fig. 6. P-marker of *Perhaps because he knew, he grinned.* The clauses *Perhaps because he past know* and *because he past know* are classified as AdvP's because they replace AdvP's (e.g., *Perhaps therefore* and *therefore*) in the matrix sentence.

Similarly in P-markers where deletion transformation has taken place a clear distinction can be made between sentence-operators and phrase-operators (fig. 7).

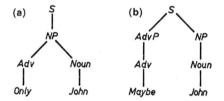

Fig. 7. P-markers with deleted VP (cf. fig. 2). In these P-markers *only* is a phrase-operator and *maybe* a sentence-operator.

To each S can only lead the path of one sentence-operating adverbial element. Thus if at the head of the sentence *Perhaps John knows* we place the adverb *Now*, this means in transformational terms that the sentence *Perhaps John knows* is embedded in the underlying matrix sentence *Now John knows*. The resultant P-marker is shown in fig. 8.

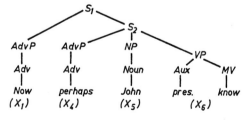

Fig. 8. P-marker of *Now perhaps John knows.*

19

The generalized transformation performing the embedding may be defined as follows:

(*Rule 2*)

Structural analysis: of S_1: AdvP–NP–VP
  of S_2: AdvP–NP–VP

Structural change: $(X_1-X_2-X_3; X_4-X_5-X_6) \Rightarrow X_1-X_4-X_5-X_6$

According to this definition the sentence *Perhaps John knows* replaces in the course of the generalized transformation the NP and VP of the sentence *Now John knows.*[22]

Under the general category *phrase-operator* many different types can be subsumed. Thus *Perhaps* in fig. 6 may be called an AdvP-operator and *Only* in fig. 7 *a* an NP-operator (notice that there is branching at the nodes marked AdvP and NP in these figures). Moreover, a useful distinction can be made between VP-operating and MV-operating adverbials, as in fig. 9. In the sentence here analysed the VP-operator *never* can very well change places with the auxiliary *was* and the MV-operator *completely* can change places with the main verb *forgotten*, but between the adverbs themselves the order is fixed (cf. Jacobson 1964, p. 35).

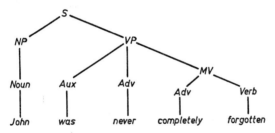

Fig. 9. P-marker with *never* as a VP-operator and *completely* as an MV-operator.

Returning now to the discussion of why functional labels are not used in transformational grammars, we may note that the feeling of their redundancy is not the only reason why they are omitted. Many functional relationships, indeed, cannot be expressed by individual P-markers. For example, the sub-configuration formed by *extremely slowly* in fig. 10 gives no indication of the

---

[22] Cf. Chomsky 1961, p. 22: "Most generalized transformations are based on elementary transformations that substitute a transformed version of the second of a pair of underlying terminal strings for some term of the proper analysis of the first of the pair."

interrelationship of these two adverbs. In order to ascertain this a set of P-markers, showing the derivational history of the adverbs, must be examined. Also, from the point of view of derivational history, it often appears that an element has more than one function.[23] For example, in the sentence *John was killed* the word *John* is subject but at the same time it is object in the underlying sentence *X killed John*.

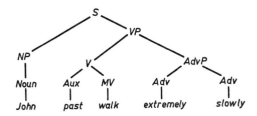

Fig. 10. P-marker of *John walked extremely slowly*.

In the type of IC-grammar where only one P-marker is used for each sentence it is very difficult to denote manifold function graphically. This applies, for instance, to the second of the following two sentences:

The industrial revolution caused great social upheaval. Especially was this the case in England.

Here the adverb *Especially* has three functions: (1) it modifies the sentence it introduces; (2) it connects this sentence with the previous sentence; (3) it directs attention to the constituent *in England*.[24] In the derivational history of the sentence, however, these functions are not simultaneous but are found at different stages of sentence-generation; therefore they can be adequately expressed by an ordered set of P-markers.

---

[23] Cf. Stockwell 1964, p. 486.
[24] Cf. Jacobson 1964, pp. 28 and 49–50.

2. A Critique of Lees's Adverbial Phrase Structure Rules

The term adverbial is defined in detail in Jacobson 1964, pp. 16 and 18–21. Suffice it here to say that under adverbial the following categories may be subsumed:

(a) all adverbs, adverbial particles, and adverb phrases, e.g. *never; out; now and then;*

(b) most prepositional phrases, e.g. *in England; by now;*

(c) many embedded sentences, e.g. *when I was young;*

(d) certain noun phrases, e.g. *(many) miles.*

An adverbialization is the process by which other elements are transformed into adverbials, and it is a question of great interest to ascertain to what extent such processes occur. The approach adopted by the present writer is that all adverbials except adverbial particles are generated by transformational rules. Lees, who has devoted some pages to the generation of adverbials both in his book *The Grammar of English Nominalizations* (see especially pp. 5–14) and in his article "The Grammatical Basis of Some Semantic Notions", is however of a different opinion. According to him at least the major types of adverbials are generated as optional elements by constituent-structure (=PS) rules, as is shown by the following enumeration of adverbial categories:[1]

"(1) *Sentence-adverbials* (Adv) which arise in the very first constituent-structure rule in an English grammar: S→Nom (Adv) VP; for example, *certainly* in the sentence: *This is certainly true.* They may be optionally and stylistically shifted to initial position: *Certainly this is true.*

(2) *Preverbs* (Prev) which arise in the second rule: VP→(Prev) Aux+MV, for example, *almost* in the sentence: *We are almost finished.* Like sentence-adverbials, their normal position is after the second member of the auxiliary in most sentence-types, and there are both affirmative and negative subtypes.[2]

---

[1] Lees 1962, pp. 13–14.

[2] When Lees says that the normal position of preverbs is "after the second member of the auxiliary" he regards the first member as the obligatory tense auxiliary that gives rise to such endings as -*s* or -*ed* in surface structure. Cf. PS rule 1 in paper no. 4.

(3) *Locative* and *Time Adverbials* (Loc and Tm) arising in the third rule

$$MV \rightarrow \begin{Bmatrix} be + Pr \\ V \end{Bmatrix} \text{ (Loc) (Tm); for example, } in\ town \text{ and } tomorrow \text{ in the}$$

sentence: *I'll meet him in town tomorrow.* Tm can also be stylistically shifted to initial position.

(4) Various *Manner Adverbials* (Man) which may follow transitive-verb objects, certain action-verbs and their complements, and intransitive verbs of certain types." (The two rules given in this context give rise to such sentences as *John explains it clearly; John became leader gradually;* and *John drives safely.* The element Man [=manner adverbial] appears within brackets to show that it is optional).

"(5) *Attributive Adverbials* (Adv$_a$) which may precede adjectives, arising originally from the expansion of the copula predicate in the rule:

$$Pr \rightarrow \begin{Bmatrix} NP \\ (Adv_a)\ Adj \\ Loc \end{Bmatrix} \text{"}$$

Some of these rules have also been adopted by Fillmore (1963, pp. 224–25). The following criticisms may, however, be levelled against them:

(1) The term *sentence-adverbial* is apparently used about adverbials which can be substituted for sentences.[3] Would it not be more correct, then, to treat them as transforms of sentences, e.g.

It is obvious that this is true ⇒ Obviously this is true

(2) The term *preverb* is based on position, as opposed to the other categories which are based on function or meaning. Apart from *almost*, Lees also mentions *scarcely*, *never*, and *not* as members of this category (Lees 1963, pp. 6, 18, and 24, respectively). But where should one draw the line? Are we to find out by statistics what adverbials appear most often in the pre-verb position and treat their other positions as transformational shifts? If *quite* belongs here, as in *I quite understand*, do *completely* and *entirely* as well, though they are quite common also after the verb (Jacobson 1964, p. 82)? In this context we may note with Schachter (1964, pp. 694–95) that in Chomsky's grammar *not* is generated by a transformational rule but in Lees's by a PS-rule (Lees 1963, p. 24; Chomsky 1957, pp. 61–62).

(3) If Lees's rule for the generation of *locative* and *time adverbials* (which is adopted by Stockwell 1960, p. 363) is correct, then the string underlying

---

[3] Cf. Kruisinga–Erades 1953, pp. 45, 92–93. On the same grounds, Bach (1964, p. 40) calls *naturally* a sentence-adverb in *That's naturally enough.*

the sentence *John went home yesterday* must have the P-marker shown by fig. 1. But is it not more probable that we have to do here with an embedding transformation? In that case the derived P-marker should be drawn as in fig. 2.

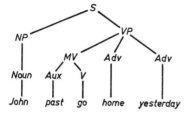

Fig. 1. P-marker with *home* and *yesterday* as VP-operators on the same level.

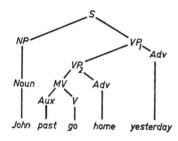

Fig. 2. P-marker with *home* and *yesterday* as VP-operators on different levels.

In fig. 1 the adverbs *home* and *yesterday* are VP-operators on the same level, whereas in fig. 2 they are so on different levels. In fig. 2 there are two underlying VP's: $VP_1 =$ "past *go yesterday*" and $VP_2 =$ "past *go home*". When VP_2 is embedded in VP_1, it replaces the MV of VP_1.

Moreover, between the adverbs *home-yesterday* and the nouns *home-day* there is an obvious connection which is overlooked by Lees's PS-rules. The connection can, however, be explicitly expressed if, instead, we let the two adverbs be generated by T-rules.

(4) Lees (1962, pp. 16–17) says that when the sentence *John drives safely* is nominalized into *John's safe driving* then the manner adverbial is shifted into its underlying adjective. But if the adverb *safely* is generated directly by PS-rules, how can it have an underlying adjective? Lees seems to be reasoning in a circle. If, on the other hand, we take the generation of *safely* to be performed by T-rules, the manner of adverbialization may be described briefly as follows: first *John drives* is nominalized into *John's driving*. Then this nominal is embedded in the sentence *Something is safe*, where it replaces the NP, the resultant sentence being *John's driving is safe*. By denominalization

24

of the NP and adverbialization of the VP this sentence yields *John drives safely*.

(5) *Attributive adverbials* may be generated by further T-rules that nominalize *John drives safely* into *John's driving safety* and then embed this nominal in the sentence *Something is extreme* so that we get the sentence *John's driving safety is extreme*, which in its turn undergoes denominalization and adverbialization into *John drives extremely safely*.

3. Notes on the Explanatory Power of Transformational Grammar

In his interesting article on transformational grammar in *Moderna språk* 4/1965 Magnus Ljung gives on p. 408 an instance of the great explanatory power of this type of grammar: "negations, affirmations and questions are merely different variations on the same underlying structure". Although this statement has to be slightly modified in the light of the most recent research in transformational grammar (see, for instance, Katz and Postal 1964, pp. 74 and 79), it is still essentially true.

The question of different levels of success for grammatical description is discussed at some length by Chomsky in chapter 2 of his book *Current Issues in Linguistic Theory*. Here he roughly delimits three such levels, viz. those of observational adequacy, descriptive adequacy, and explanatory adequacy. The problem of achieving explanatory adequacy in transformational grammars he says is that of formulating a general condition on the construction of such grammars so that they not only give a correct description of the output of a speaker's linguistic intuition but also an explanation of the functioning of this intuition. The attainment of such explanatory adequacy is a very great goal which cannot be reached without the observation of a rigorously applied technique involving frequent use of symbols and formulas. Sometimes, however, these have the disadvantage of making an exposition heavy, at least for a reader whose knowledge of mathematics or symbolic logic is limited. The difficulties that have to be overcome tend to obscure the fact that transformational grammar has a power to describe and explain intricate grammatical problems that often greatly exceeds that of other grammatical systems. In the present article I will try to give a few instances of this explanatory power without using the customary amount of formulaic language. Thus I will not describe the technical side of performing the various transformations but only discuss them in oversimplified and thus, I hope, more intelligible form.

A pair of examples frequently used to emphasize the value of the transformational approach are the following:[1]

John is easy to please.

John is eager to please.

Traditional grammar might explain the difference between these sentences by saying that in the first *John* is the logical object of *please*, whereas in the second it is its logical subject. Though entirely correct, this explanation, however, really requires further exposition to be clearly understood by anyone hearing it for the first time. Evidently these sentences have an unexpressed semantic content which traditional grammar is well aware of but hesitates to describe in the form of explicit strings; it seems as if it is only in the case of obvious ellipses that traditional grammar feels free to supply suppressed words. Transformational grammar has no such hesitation; on the contrary, one of its main objects is to describe the abstract structures that are felt to underlie the sentences actually produced in the act of linguistic performance. Thus in the deep structure underlying *John is easy to please* a transformational description assumes the presence of the string *to please John* and in that underlying *John is eager to please* the string *John pleases someone*.[2]

In a discussion held at Uppsala University on a recent thesis by Carlehäll (Carlehäll 1966), I took the opportunity to point out how the great explanatory power of transformational grammar can be utilized to give a clear and explicit account of certain intricate syntactic relationships.

One interesting problem was this: why is *will* used to denote pure future in the conditional clause of the following example:[3]

If it won't bore you, I'll show you some more of my work.

Traditional grammar usually states that in such cases the conditional clause should have the present tense since it is sufficient to express the idea

---

[1] See Chomsky 1964*b*, p. 34.

[2] The object can also be some other word or phrase that suits the semantic context, or it can be an abstract dummy element, i.e. the designated representative of the category that is deleted (cf. Chomsky 1964*b*, p. 41). The relationship between a deletion and an ellipsis may be described as follows: a deletion is an elementary transformation whose result in surface structure often, but far from always, appears in the form of an ellipsis. The term ellipsis is here understood in the way it is defined by *Webster's Third New International Dictionary*: "Omission of one or more words that are obviously understood but must be supplied to make a construction grammatically complete."

[3] See Carlehäll 1966, p. 48.

of futurity only in the main clause.[4] While therefore this type of grammar has to treat the above sentence as an exceptional case, transformational grammar can approach the problem in a different manner by reckoning with deep structure elements that are deleted by transformations. Thus the underlying structure on which the semantic content of the surface structure is based may be represented as follows:

If you are sure (if you think, etc.) that it won't bore you if I do so, I'll show you some more of my work.

Here we first recognize a conditional clause ("If you think") preceding a main clause ("I'll show you some more of my work"). Embedded in the *if*-clause is a *that*-clause, which in its turn contains another *if*-clause ("If I do so"). As we see, *will* here occurs not in an *if*-clause but in a *that*-clause, i.e. in a clause-type where it is found quite frequently as an expression of pure futurity.[5]

This way of interpreting the presence of *will* denoting pure future in surface structure *if*-clauses bears a certain resemblance to the way in which Chomsky explains the problem why a reflexive pronoun is used in *I aimed it at myself* but a personal pronoun in *I kept it near me* (Chomsky 1965, p. 146). Chomsky says that the second sentence has a deep structure which in over-simplified form may be rendered as *I kept it. It was near me*, whereas the first sentence has a deep structure of the form *I aimed it at me*, i.e. there is no underlying sentence of the form *It was at me*. The reflexivization rule that transforms *me* in *I aimed it at me* into *myself* does not operate in *I kept it. It was near me*, as in this case *me* is not coreferent with the subject.

Though I have so far tried to refrain from indulging in the symbolic language used by most transformationists, I should like to give a hint of the explanatory power that inheres in the phrase-markers that are used in transformational grammars. We may, for instance, ask ourselves what basic structural similarity or difference there is between the following noun phrases:[6]

(*a*) Jack's father's uncle's house.

(*b*) The man you introduced me to from Stockholm who was a teacher.

(*c*) The man who built the house that has a roof which is green.

---

[4] See, for instance, Jespersen 1933, § 23.4₃.

[5] A traditional grammar like Gabrielson 1950, § 237, has a similar explanation, but uses terms of the type "implicit" or "understood" for what is a strictly formalized and explicit deep structure in transformational grammar. (This footnote was added in 1970.)

[6] For other similar examples see Chomsky 1965, p. 13.

The tree diagrams in fig. 1 can better than any words clarify the various types of structure.

(a)

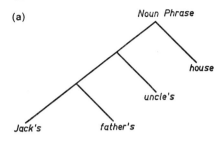

(b)

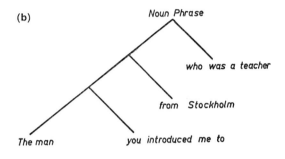

(c)

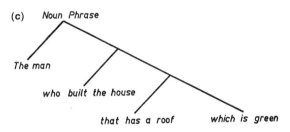

Fig. 1. Left-branching trees (*a* and *b*) and a right-branching tree (*c*).

These notes on the explanatory power of transformational grammar should not be regarded as a claim that this type of grammar is in all respects new and superior to all other types of grammatical description. Its links with both traditional grammar and other modern schools are obvious. This is clearly demonstrated by H. A. Gleason, Jr., in some chapters of his book *Linguistics*

29

and English Grammar. Gleason discusses three types of generative grammar and shows that each of them is related to some basic technique of description that has earlier been used in English grammar. The first type is essentially equivalent to the immediate-constituent analysis of structural grammar and the second to the slot-and-filler technique used by, for instance, the tagmemic school (Gleason 1965, pp. 243 and 248–49). The third type leaves modifiers to be generated by the transformational component of the grammar, i.e. modifiers are hung on to structures rather than regarded as constituting an integral part of them. This third type, says Gleason (p. 289), is reminiscent of the base-and-modifier technique of school grammar and of some traditional grammars. Gleason's chapters on generative grammar are a very instructive and highly commendable attempt to demonstrate that in the development of grammatical theory the proponents of new schools are not so independent of earlier grammatical methods as some people tend to think.

4. Some Aspects of Preverbs

1. S and VP Operating Preverbs[1]

From the point of view of generation it is possible to distinguish two types of adverbs which can occur in surface structure between NP (=noun phrase) and V (=verb) and which, when they are in this position, are suitably termed preverbs.[2] In phrase-markers these adverbs are immediately dominated by the node S (=sentence) or by the node VP (=verb phrase) and may thus be termed S-operating and VP-operating preverbs, respectively. Although not really placed before a verb, adverbs occurring between NP and Pred (=predicative) are also included in the former category if they are immediately dominated by the node S. Fig. 1 gives phrase-marker illustrations of the two categories.

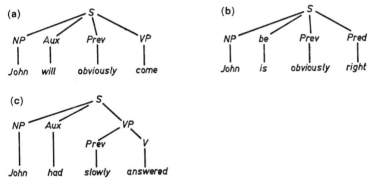

Fig. 1. Simplified derived phrase-markers with an S-operating preverb (*a* and *b*) and a VP-operating preverb (*c*). S =sentence, NP =noun phrase, Aux = auxiliary, Prev =preverb, VP =verb phrase, Pred =predicative, V =verb.

---

[1] In the opinion of Owen Thomas, "the preverbs, as a group, are the least understood subclass of adverbs" (Thomas 1966: 163).

[2] In transformational grammar the term preverb is used for adverbs such as *always, ever, seldom, almost, hardly,* which usually occur between NP and V (cf. Thomas 1966: 163). Consistency would have required the use of positional terms also for other types of adverbs, but so far I have not found terms like "postverbs" or "interverbs" used by transformationalists. The reader should note that in the present work "preverb" is used as a strictly positional term (=adverb in mid-position).

A description will now be given of how some major categories of S-operating and VP-operating preverbs may be generated. For this purpose the following derivation of S will be used:

PS-rule 1

$$S \quad \rightarrow NP + Aux \begin{Bmatrix} be + Pred \\ VP \end{Bmatrix} (Seq)$$

NP $\rightarrow Det + N$ (S)

Aux $\rightarrow Tn$ (M) (Perf)

$$Tn \quad \rightarrow \begin{Bmatrix} Pres \\ Past \end{Bmatrix}$$

M $\rightarrow can, will,$ etc.

Perf $\rightarrow have + en$

$$VP \quad \rightarrow \begin{Bmatrix} V \ (NP) \\ Cop + Nom \end{Bmatrix} (Seq)$$

Cop $\rightarrow become,$ etc.

$$Nom \rightarrow \begin{Bmatrix} NP \\ Adj \end{Bmatrix}$$

$$Pred \rightarrow \begin{Bmatrix} Nom \\ Advl \end{Bmatrix}$$

Seq $\rightarrow$ S

Abbreviations

PS	phrase structure
Seq	sequence sentence
Det	determiner
N	noun
Tn	tense
M	modal
Perf	perfect
Pres	present
Cop	copula
Nom	nominal
Adj	adjective
Advl	adverbial

The derivation of Aux is based on an amendment suggested by Michael Grady, who does not include the progressive aspect in Aux, as earlier transformationalists do,[3] but assumes that all *ing*-forms are to be generated by a special nominalization transformation (Grady 1967: 6–7). According to Grady's theory the surface structure sentence *The boy is singing* has the underlying structure of fig. 2.

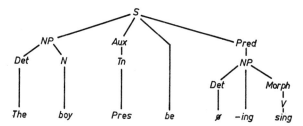

Fig. 2. The generation of progressive forms according to Grady.

---

[3] See, for example, Chomsky 1965: 43 and Thomas 1966: 130.

A derivation of this type obviates such ungrammatical sentences as

*John may have been being right.
*Jane must be being a good cook.

which might be generated according to the following earlier formula:

PS-rule 2

$$VP \rightarrow Aux \begin{Bmatrix} be + \text{Pred} \\ V \end{Bmatrix}$$

$$Aux \rightarrow \text{Tense (Modal)} \ (have + en) \ (be + ing)$$

The derivation of S in PS-rule 1 as

$$S \rightarrow NP + Aux \begin{Bmatrix} be + \text{Pred} \\ VP \end{Bmatrix} \text{(Seq)}$$

is my own innovation. It makes it possible to attach preverbs inserted between *be* and Pred to the node S, as in fig. 1*b*. This would not have been the case if *be* + Pred had been a rewriting of VP or MV (= main verb), as in Chomsky 1965: 102 or Thomas 1966: 98–99. The symbol Seq denotes a sequence sentence which is optional and therefore enclosed in brackets.

1.1. *Examples of the generation of S-operating preverbs*

According to Chomsky 1965: 100–01, sentence-operating adverbs in -*ly* may be generated from underlying strings with NP's of the form *it* + S. Thomas (1966: 162–63) has a similar derivation, but instead of *it* he more abstractly speaks of PRO-forms of Det + N (as regards PRO-forms see Thomas 1966: 87–90). A matter unaccounted for in both cases is how the sentence which underlies the adverb becomes embedded, for it is obvious that the adverb, as a modifier, is subordinate to the rest of the sentence in

Obviously John can come.
John can come, obviously.,

whereas, if adverbialization does not take place, it is the other sentence that is embedded and thus becomes subordinate:

It is obvious that John can come.

A conceivable solution seems to be to assume that we have here not two underlying sentences but three; then the difference in subordination is easily accounted for as due to deletion of different underlying sentences. Thus in fig. 3, which shows the deep structure of *John can come, obviously*, S₃ is deleted. This deletion is possible because S_3 and S_1, apart from Seq, are identical (cf. Chomsky 1965: 138). If, on the other hand, we remove the adverbialization morpheme *-ly* from the deep structure in fig. 3, we will after various transformations arrive at the surface structure *It is obvious that John can come*, i.e. S_1 is deleted, whereas S_3 remains.

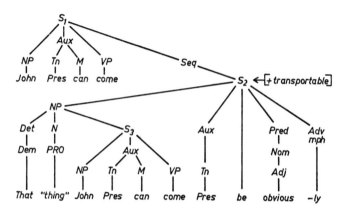

Fig. 3. The deep structure of *John can come, obviously*.

The word that connects the sequence sentence S_2 with the independent sentence S_1 is the demonstrative determiner *that*. In the case of adverbialization this is always deleted, but in the parallel case with *It is*+adj. in the surface structure its deletion is optional, as we can have both

It is obvious that John can come.
and
It is obvious John can come.

The adverbialization caused by the morpheme *-ly* involves deletion of NP, Aux, and *be* of S_2, leaving only *obvious* and *-ly*, which thus come to be immediately dominated by the node S_1.

According to the transportability convention proposed by S. J. Keyser (1967: 52–53), the node that immediately dominates an adverb whose place in the sentence is not fixed should be marked with the feature [+transportable]. Earlier it was considered impossible to attach such a feature to a syntactic node like S, as features, according to Chomsky 1965: 79–81, could specify only lexical formatives, i.e. they belonged to subcategorization, not to branching. In Chomsky 1967: 31 it is suggested, however, that "certain features should be associated with nonlexical phrase categories". I have therefore attached the feature [+transportable] to S_2, thereby denoting that S_2 and the adverb into which it is transformed can be placed before or after all other nodes immediately dominated by S_1. We thus obtain the set of derived phrase-markers illustrated by fig. 4a–d, the last two of which show *obviously* as a preverb.

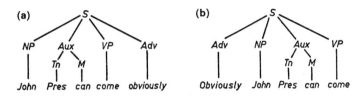

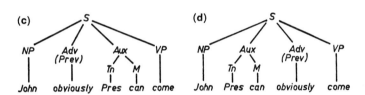

Fig. 4. Derived phrase-markers illustrating the transportability of an S-operating adverb.

In the derivation of S in PS-rule 1 Aux has been treated as indivisible in relation to S. The fact, however, that we can put an S-operating preverb in the following position

John can obviously have come.

indicates that in cases where both M and Perf are selected in the derivation of Aux one has to reckon with two parts of Aux, each immediately dominated by S. I will call these Aux_1 and Aux_2. A survey of the various realizations of Aux, Aux_1, and Aux_2 is given in table 1, and fig. 5 shows a derived phrase-marker with Aux_1 and Aux_2.

Table I. *Various realizations of Aux*

PS-rules	Examples of result in surface structure
$Aux \rightarrow \begin{cases} Tn \\ Tn + M \\ Tn + Perf \end{cases}$	*-s, Ø, -ed* *can, could* *has, have, had*
$Aux_1 \rightarrow Tn + M$ $Aux_2 \rightarrow Perf$	$\Big\}$ *could have*

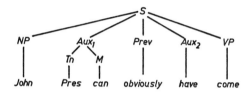

Fig. 5. Derived phrase-marker with Aux_1 and Aux_2.

Generalized phrase-markers similar to that of fig. 3 can probably also be used in the generation of certain other adverbs not ending in *-ly*. Thus we can change fig. 3 so that the last two nodes of S_2 look as in fig. 6. This deep structure can then be regarded as the basis of those derived phrase-markers which would form part of the derivational history of such surface structure sentences as

John can come now.
Now John can come.
John now can come. $\Big\}$ Preverbial
John can now come. $\Big\}$ instances

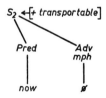

Fig. 6. The change needed to make fig. 3 show the deep structure of *John can come now.*

Just as fig. 3 without the adverbialization morpheme would give *It is obvious that John can come*, where the predicative adjective *obvious* is retained, so the originally predicative *now* seems to survive in such sentences as

The right moment is now.
The meeting is not tomorrow; the meeting is now.

Here *now* may be compared with a locative word used predicatively, as in *John is here.*

1.1.1. In this derivation of the adverb *now* a transformationalist position is adopted, i.e. the end-product in surface structure is assumed to be attained by transformations. Another, and perhaps in some respects preferable, approach is the lexicalist one, according to which *now* would be inserted directly as an S-operating adverb with a set of features such as [+transportable, +temporal, etc.].[4]

In his recent work on nominalizations Chomsky (1967: 5) says that it is "quite possible to imagine a compromise solution that adopts the lexicalist position for certain items and the transformationalist for others". This statement seems to be applicable also to the generation of preverbs, for we have, on the one extreme, the regular derivation with adjective + *ly*, and on the other, all kinds of *ad hoc* formations, such as *again, already, doubtless, forever, maybe, often, seldom, soon*, and *yet*. In between these there are certain small groups of preverbs with the same or at least similar derivation, e.g. (1) *here, hence*, (2) *there, then, thus*, (3) *anyhow, somehow*, (4) *somewhere, everywhere, nowhere*. One group consists of preverbs of the same form as the corresponding adjective, i.e. they can be derived transformationally in the same way as *obviously* in fig. 3 but with a zero adverb morpheme, e.g. *best, first, last, long, sure.*

1.2. *Examples of the generation of VP-operating preverbs*

VP-operating adverbs in *-ly* may be generated in a way which resembles that of S-operating adverbs. As can be seen in fig. 7, which is an attempt to illustrate the deep structure of *John jokes wildly*, the major difference is that

---

[4] If a sentence into which *now* is inserted is in the past tense, the feature [+sequence-signalling] must also be added, for *now* then refers to an implied or specified time, as in "The meeting was postponed till 8 p.m. and now John could come". For a further discussion of sequence-signalling, see 3.2.

the sequence sentence S_2 is attached not to the S-node of S_1 but to the VP-node, for it is only the verb *joke* that is involved.

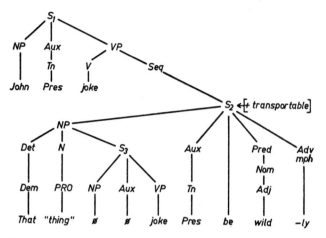

Fig. 7. The deep structure of *John jokes wildly.*

The adverbialization morpheme causes deletion of the whole of S_2 except *wild* and *-ly*, which thus come to be immediately dominated by the node VP of S_1. This transformational procedure bypasses the verb-nominalization assumed by Thomas (1966: 169), who admits, however, that his description

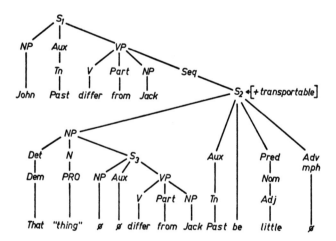

Fig. 8. The deep structure of *John little differed from Jack.* Part = particle (as regards its VP-operating function, see Jacobson 1966: 119–21.

is only tentative, as "more work needs to be done on the precise form of this transformation in a scientific grammar".

According to the transportability convention the VP-operating adverb can be placed before or after the V. It is in the former position that it may be called a preverb and as such it automatically follows all Aux elements and S-operating preverbs (see 2.2.B.2 and fig. 14). When a VP-operating adverb is placed after the V, its position has to be considered in relation to a possible adverbial particle and/or a VP-operating NP (Keyser 1967: 54 ff.).

Not only adverbs in -ly may be generated in the manner shown by fig. 7 but probably also others, e.g. *little* in the sentence *John little differed from Jack*, which seems to be based on a generalized phrase-marker of the type shown in fig. 8.

2. Preverbial Positions

Preverbs may be classified according to the position in which they occur. In finite constructions this is always some kind of mid-position. In Jacobson 1964, chapter II, mid-position was defined as any position between two or more of the elements S, T, v, and P,[5] irrespective of their order in relation to each other. As many as eight subdivisions of mid-position, denoted M1–M8 could be differentiated.

I will here deal only with preverbs which in surface structure occur in sentences with normal word-order, i.e. where NP precedes VP or *be* + Pred, and in corresponding sentences with anticipatory *there*.[6] This restriction excludes the rather rare positions M5 and M7, as in

M5 Among the greatest, *undoubtedly*, was poverty.

M7 By this term is meant, *presumably*, the ability to image an absent scene ...[7]

Furthermore, no special treatment is considered necessary for cases whose deep-structure generation includes a rule of this type:

---

[5] S = subject; T = anticipatory *there*; v = auxiliary or copula of simple or compound form; P = main verb or copula complement.

[6] In *there*-constructions with *there* + *be* + NP, NP corresponds to Pred in *be* + Pred constructions. Adverbs placed between *there* and this NP are therefore also regarded as preverbs. For a description of the transformation that introduces *there*, see Chomsky 1967: 32–33 and n. 33.

[7] For the sources of these two examples, see Jacobson 1964: 320 and 357.—Though M7 can be classed as a type of mid-position on the basis of the definition given above, it is not a preverbial position, as the adverb here occurs *after* v + VP or Pred.

PS-rule 3
S   →NP+Aux+VP
Aux→Tn

If an adverb is inserted between NP and VP in such a sentence, it will occupy the very common position M1, as in

M1 John *obviously* joked.
    John *little* differed from Jack.

Interest is instead focussed on how preverbs are placed in relation to such manifestations of Aux as M and Perf and in relation to forms of *be*.[8] In these cases we can distinguish between pre- and post-auxiliary placement in a way which is not possible when Aux only indicates whether the tense is the present or the past.

Positions M2, M3, M4, M6 and M8 will now, wherever applicable, be defined for two different types of sentences:

    1. Sentences directly based on PS-rule 1 (incl. the Aux rules in table 1).
    2. Various transforms of these basic sentences.

2.1. *Position M2*

Only S-operating preverbs occur in M2.
    1. In basic sentences M2 is the position of a preverb placed before Aux, (*a*) when Aux is followed by *be*+Pred, (*b*) when Aux is followed by VP and is rewritten as Tn+M, Tn+Perf, or Tn+M+Perf. For examples of derived phrase-markers with a preverb in M2 see figures 4*c* and 9, which give the following surface structure sentences, respectively:

John *obviously* is right (9*a*).
John *obviously* can come (4*c*).
John *obviously* must have come (9*b*).

    2. In transforms the same rules obtain as under 1, whenever applicable, but M2 is also the case before Aux, (*a*) when Aux is followed by *be*+V+*ing* in progressive constructions, by *be*+V+*en* in passive constructions, and by *be*+NP in *there*-constructions, (*b*) when Aux is followed by *do* in negative and emphatic constructions. Examples:

---

[8] Note that the abbreviation M by itself means modal auxiliary, whereas M1, M2, etc. denote various subdivisions of mid-position.

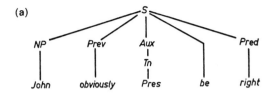

(a)

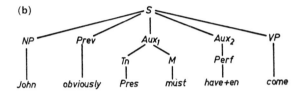

(b)

Fig. 9, Derived phrase-markers of *John obviously is right* (*a*) and *John obviously must have come* (*b*).

Progressive:	John *probably* is working.
	John *probably* must have been working.
Passive:	John *never* was caught.
	John *never* has been caught.
There-*construction:*	There *always* is a chance.
	There *always* might be a chance.
Negative:	John *usually* does not sing.
Emphatic:	John *usually* does sing.

According to fig. 2, *be* + V + *ing* in progressive constructions is based on *be* + Pred and thus has the same *be* as the latter.

Passive constructions, too, may be generated transformationally from *be* + Pred, the latter category being rewritten as an NP containing an embedded sentence of the form NP + Aux + V + NP + AgP. Thus the surface structure sentence *The man was caught by the police* might be based on the generalized phrase-marker in fig. 10 and the derived phrase-marker in fig. 11.

The Aux of S_2 in fig. 10 is realized as a nominalization morpheme, *en,*[9] which is added to the V of S_2 to change it into a past participle. Any verb inserted from the lexicon to replace this V must, like *catch*, have the feature

---

[9] According to Chomsky 1967, n. 6, Tn (M) can be replaced by various nominalization elements.

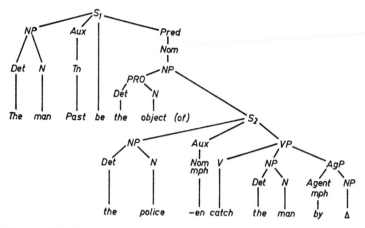

Fig. 10. The deep structure of *The man was caught by the police.* Nom mph = nominalization morpheme, AgP = agent phrase, Δ = dummy symbol (cf. Chomsky 1965: 122 and 1967: 28).

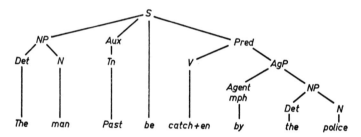

Fig. 11. Derived phrase-marker of *The man was caught by the police.*

[+passive] (Svartvik 1967 and cf. Chomsky 1967: 27). The surface structure generated by the phrase-marker in fig. 10 has an explicit agent, but if the first NP of S_2 had been PRO, the agent morpheme, too, would have been realized as PRO, and the result in surface structure would have been an agentless sentence: *The man was caught.*

Apart from the nominalization of V into a past participle, the passivization transformation involves substitution of the first NP of S_2 ("the police") for Δ and deletion of the second NP of S_2 ("the man") as this NP has its exact counterpart in S_1. Moreover, in S_1 the words *the object (of)*, which are purely functional in that they only denote the relationship between S_1 and S_2, can be regarded as a type of PRO and are as such deletable.

This approach to passivization explains an important point that has so far, to my knowledge, been left unexplained, namely how the active verb is changed into a form of *be* + a past participle.[10]

If, as is the case in this description, the *by*-agent is thought of as being a Pred-operator in a derived phrase-marker (fig. 11), it is natural for its position to be quite fixed in relation to V, which is actually the case in surface structure, for we hardly find

*By the police the man was caught.
*The man by the police was caught.
*The man was by the police caught.

As a matter of fact, the position of the agent is much more fixed than that of manner adverbials in general (cf. Jacobson 1964: 89). According to Svartvik (1967: 2), it is debatable whether all agents really are to be classified as manner adverbials.

Most *there*-constructions are also to be derived from *be* + Pred with Pred rewritten as Advl with the feature [+locative]. For example, the sentence *There are two boys in the room* goes back to *Two boys are in the room*. Occasionally *there*-constructions show other types of derivation, e.g.

Be + *adjectival Pred:* There are now available several books which deal with this problem.

Be *as VP or* **be** + *deleted Pred:* There are children who always have to go to bed hungry.

Active VP: There will doubtless come a time when they will regret this decision.

Passive VP: There has recently been developed a machine which produces a "voiceprint" (GLG 354).

In the negative and emphatic transforms *do* takes the place of M if the sentence contains no modal auxiliary. It is, however, never followed by Perf and only in the imperative by *be*.

---

[10] Chomsky (1967: 26) describes passivization as follows: "Let us suppose ... that the underlying structure for passives is roughly NP-Aux-V-NP by A, where by A is an agent phrase related, in ways that are still unclear in detail, to adverbials of means and manner. The passive operation, then, is an amalgam of two steps: the first replaces A by the subject noun phrase; the second inserts in the position vacated by the subject the noun phrase that is to the right of the verb."

43

2.2. Position M3

Both S-operating and VP-operating preverbs occur in M3.

    A. S-operators

    1. In basic sentences M3 is the position of a preverb placed (*a*) after Aux + *be*, when Aux is rewritten as Tn (fig. 12*a*), (*b*) after Aux when Aux is rewritten as Tn + M or Tn + Perf (figs. 4*d* and 12*b*), (*c*) after Tn + M (= Aux$_1$), when Aux is rewritten as Tn + M + Perf (fig. 5).

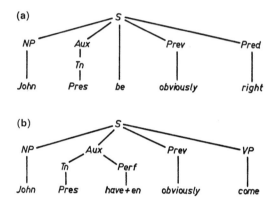

Fig. *12*. Derived phrase-markers of *John is obviously right* (*a*) and *John has obviously come* (*b*).

    2. In transforms the same rules apply as under 1 with the addition that M3 is also the case after Aux + *do* in negative and emphatic constructions. Examples:

Progressive:	John is *probably* working.
	John must *probably* have been working.
Passive:	John was *never* caught.
	John has *never* been caught.
There-*construction:*	There is *always* a chance.
	There might *always* be a chance.
Negative:	John does not *often* sing.
Emphatic:	John does *indeed* sing.[11]

---

[11] Cf. the following example from BSP 205: "I looked at the faded picture of his faded family and did *indeed* see what he meant."

B. VP-operators

1. In basic sentences M3 is the position of a preverb placed between Aux and V, when Aux is rewritten as Tn+M or Tn+Perf (fig. 13).[12]

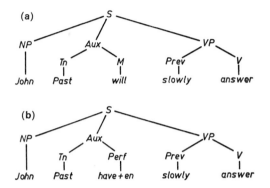

Fig. 13. Derived phrase-markers of *John would slowly answer* (*a*) and *John had slowly answered* (*b*).

2. In transforms the same rule applies as above under 1 with the addition that M3 is also the case (*a*) between *be* and V in progressive and passive constructions when Aux is rewritten as Tn, (*b*) between Tn+*do* and V in negative and emphatic constructions.[13] Examples:

Progressive:　John was *slowly* rising.

Passive:　John was *little* affected.

Negative:　John does not *much* differ from Jack.

Emphatic:　I do *so* like children. (so = very much)

Whenever an S-operating preverb and a VP-operating preverb stand together in M3, the former always precedes the latter, for in mid-position a node immediately dominated by S must precede a node immediately dominated by VP. See fig. 14, which illustrates the order between the two preverbs *obviously* and *little*.

---

[12] M3 can also be the position between Aux and Cop as in "They have *openly* turned Catholic."

[13] V can in these transforms, except in the passive, be replaced by Cop, as in "It was *slowly* getting dark", "He did (not) *openly* turn Catholic".

45

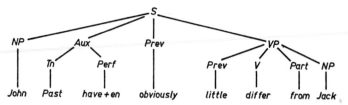

Fig. 14. Derived phrase-marker of *John had obviously little differed from Jack.*

2.3. *Position M4*

M4 is a position mainly occupied by VP-operating preverbs; only occasionally do S-operators occur here.

A. S-operators

1. In basic sentences M4 is the position of a preverb placed (*a*) after Aux + *be* when Aux is rewritten as Tn + M, Tn + Perf, or Tn + M + Perf (fig. 15*a*), (*b*) between Aux₂ and VP (fig. 15*b*).

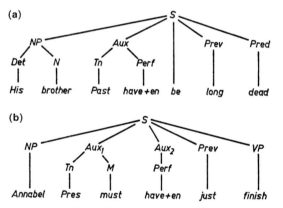

Fig. 15. Derived phrase-markers of *His brother had been long dead* (*a*) and *Annabel must have just finished* (*b*).[14]

2. In transforms the same rules apply as under 1. In the following examples no negative and emphatic transforms are illustrated, as periphrastic *do* does not co-occur with M or Perf:[15]

---

[14] For a fuller version of these two sentences see JHA 131 and JHA 120. Phrase-markers similar to that of fig. 15*a* can be drawn for *His brother must be long dead* (Tn + M) and *His brother must have been long dead* (Tn + M + Perf). In fig. 15*b just* means "only a short time ago".

[15] For the full context of the examples see TSO 68, JUR 117, HWC 87, and WOM 12, respectively.

Progressive: ... she was being *sometimes* cruel.
                       ... he'd be *forever* sitting.[16]
Passive: ... a bunk which had been *recently* welded.
There-*construction:* There should be, *then*, no conflict between man and
                       society.

B. VP-operators

1. In basic sentences M4 is the position of a preverb placed between Aux_2 and V (fig. 16).

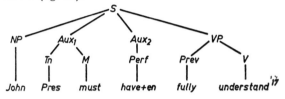

Fig. 16. Derived phrase-marker of *John must have fully understood*.

2. In transforms the same rule applies as above under 1 with the addition that M4 is also the case between *be* and V in progressive and passive constructions when Aux is rewritten as $Tn + M$, $Tn + Perf$, or $Tn + M + Perf$. Examples:

Progressive: The enemy may be *slowly* advancing $(Tn + M)$.
          The enemy has been *slowly* advancing $(Tn + Perf)$.
          The enemy may have been *slowly* advancing $(Tn + M + Perf)$.[18]
Passive: The enemy must be *thoroughly* defeated $(Tn + M)$.
          The enemy has been *thoroughly* defeated $(Tn + Perf)$.
          The enemy must have been *thoroughly defeated* $(Tn + M + Perf)$.

2.4. *Position M6*

Only S-operators occur in this very rare position.
1. In basic sentences M6 is the position of a preverb placed between Aux_2 and *be* (fig. 17).

---

[16] A contracted finite Aux (Aux_1) seems to be a contributory factor when S-operators are placed in M4. Other examples: "I'd have *probably* started" (JHA 168), "You've been *recently* dreaming walking down the street" (TVR 45).
[17] V can be replaced by Cop, e.g. "He cannot have *openly* turned Catholic". Note that the present book differs from Jacobson 1964 as regards the designation of preverbial positions in relation to Cop.
[18] In progressive constructions V can be replaced by Cop, e.g. "It has been *slowly* getting dark".

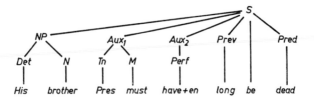

Fig. 17. Derived phrase-marker of *His brother must have long been dead.*

2. In transforms the same rule applies as above under 1. Examples:

Progressive: The enemy must have *long* been advancing.

Passive: ... the Indians would have *ultimately* been crushed (HAI 94).

There-*construction:* There must have *long* been disagreement between them.

2.5. *Position M8*

A. S-operators

When a sentence containing a preverb is transformed into a *there*-construction where NP precedes VP or Pred, the preverb usually retains its position in relation to Aux and *be*, as in

Children are *now* coming to manhood who never saw a London fog ⇒ There are *now* children coming to manhood who never saw a London fog.

This position of *now* has been defined above as a type of M3. Occasionally, however, the preverb is placed in M8, which is the position between NP and VP or Pred:

There are children *now* coming to manhood who never saw a London fog.[19]

B. VP-operators

Placement of a VP-operating preverb in M8 between NP and V or Cop is regularly the case when a sentence with such a preverb in M3 or M4 is transformed into the kind of *there*-construction where NP is followed by VP, e.g.

Near the jetty a sailing-boat was (had been) *quietly* lying at anchor ⇒ Near the jetty there was (had been) a sailingboat *quietly* lying at anchor.

---

[19] For the source and full context of this example with M8, see Jacobson 1964: 65.

48

2.6. *Diagnostic key*

M2, which is the only one of the positions illustrated in fig. 18 that occurs before Tn, is suitably termed *pre-auxiliary mid-position*.

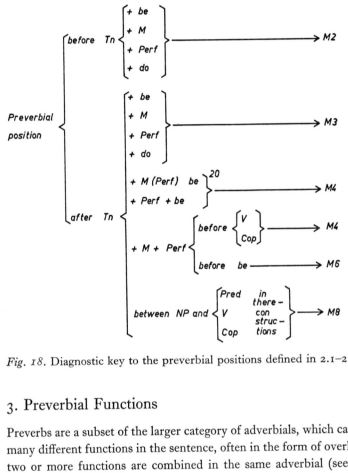

Fig. 18. Diagnostic key to the preverbial positions defined in 2.1–2.5.

3. Preverbial Functions

Preverbs are a subset of the larger category of adverbials, which can perform many different functions in the sentence, often in the form of overlap so that two or more functions are combined in the same adverbial (see Jacobson 1964: 28–52). From a functional point of view, then, preverbs can be divided into the following classes:

1. Pure modifiers.
2. Modifiers which also serve as sequence-signals.[21]

---

[20] The brackets round Perf denote that it is an optional element.
[21] Called "conjunctive adverbs" in Jacobson 1964. Note that pure sequence-signals are not adverbs but conjunctions.

3. Modifiers which also serve as focalizers.[22]
4. Modifiers which also serve as sequence-signals and focalizers.

The following two adverbial classes, which do not comprise words which are preverbs according to the definition given in 1, par. 1, will also be included in the discussion below for the sake of comparison: (1) pure focalizers, (2) focalizers which also serve as sequence-signals.

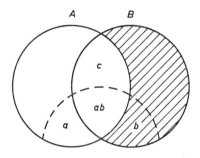

Fig. 19. The relationship between various functions performed by preverbs.

Fig. 19 represents the *relationship* between the various functions mentioned above. No indication of quantity is intended; thus the size of the different independent or overlapping areas does not reflect the number of items that belong to the various classes. Set A consists of modifiers and set B of focalizers. Each of them has a subset consisting of sequence-signals (*a* and *b*). They also have an intersection which is divided into two halves. In the upper part of the intersection (*c*) are those preverbs which are both modifiers and focalizers and in the lower part (*ab*) those which besides being modifiers and focalizers are also sequence-signals. The shaded area of *B* denotes either pure focalizers or, in its lower part (*b*), focalizers which also serve as sequence-signals.

3.1. *Pure Modification (Class 1)*

Most preverbs serve as pure modifiers. From the point of view of derivational history preverbial modification is a deep-structure function, i.e. it belongs to base phrase-markers, in the case of those preverbs which are inserted directly from the lexicon (see 1.1.1). With the use of the notational

---

[22] Called "referential adverbs" in Jacobson 1964.

system introduced by Chomsky (1965: 68–71) the notion preverbial modifier may in this case be defined as follows:

$$\text{Preverbial Modifier-of: } \left[\text{Preverb, } \left\{ \begin{array}{l} \text{S} \\ be + \text{Pred} \\ \text{VP} \end{array} \right\} \right]$$

This formula, which means that a preverb directly dominated by S, be + Pred, or VP is a preverbial modifier, is analogous to earlier definitions of the type "A sentence-modifier modifies the sentence in which it stands (i.e. it is itself an integral part of the modified sentence)".

In the case of transformationally derived preverbs, for example those derived by means of the generalized phrase-markers in figs. 3 and 7, one might say that the modifying function is performed in the deep structure by the sequence sentence from which they are derived. This situation is comparable to that of adjectival modifiers in noun phrases, e.g. *a rich man*, where the modifying function is performed in the deep structure by an embedded sentence of the form NP + Aux + be + Pred (Thomas 1965: 92).

Pure modification is the function of all preverbs exemplified in the previous section on Preverbial Positions (except *then* in 2.3, A2, which belongs to class 2).

3.2. *Modification + Sequence-signalling (Class 2)*

Modifiers which also serve as sequence-signals have the characteristic that they point either forward to a following sentence or backward to a preceding one, the latter of these two alternatives being much more common than the former. Like pure modifiers they can be derived transformationally or inserted directly from the lexicon. For example, a backward-pointing preverb such as *then* in the context "They had played. They had then returned." may be generated transformationally in the manner indicated by the somewhat simplified generalized phrase-marker in fig. 20.

In this phrase-marker *then* is derived in the same way as *now* in figs. 3 and 6, i.e. *then* is described as being generated by a transportable sequence sentence (S_3), in which it has a predicative function. The reference backward to S_1 is achieved by repeating S_1 within a relative sentence (S_4), which is later deleted when it has served its purpose. The symbol # in a ring is used in fig. 20 as an intonation morpheme that indicates where the surface structure sentences will end.

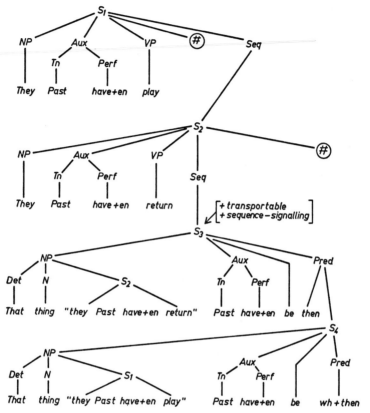

Fig. 20. The deep structure of *They had played. They had then returned.*

For easier comprehension the content of fig. 20 may be read as follows: "They had played. They had returned. Their return had taken place then when they had played." The fact that S_2 is a sequence sentence of S_1 here gives *then* the meaning "soon after the time".

A string of the same form as $S_3 + S_4$ is also to be found in the generalized phrase-marker that underlies the surface structure "When they had played, they had returned". In the transformational process, however, it is in this case S_3 containing the word *then* that is deleted, not its relative *when*-sentence (fig. 21).

Sequence-signalling modifiers are usually S-operators, as in the case of *then* in fig. 20, but they can also be VP-operators as in the case of *correspondingly* in "If a person earns more money, his taxes will correspondingly increase".

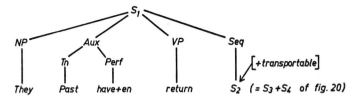

Fig. 21. The deep structure of *When they had played, they had returned.*

3.3. Modification + Focalization (Class 3)

Modifiers which also serve as focalizers are generated in the same way as pure modifiers with the addition that they, or the sequence sentences from which they are derived, have the feature [+focalizing]. Moreover, the sentence element which is focussed has the feature [+focus] and is given emphatic stress and intonation in the phonological component. Thus the sentence *John had primarily spoken of Kate*, where the preverb *primarily* focusses the noun *Kate*, may be based on the partly simplified generalized phrase-marker in fig. 22.

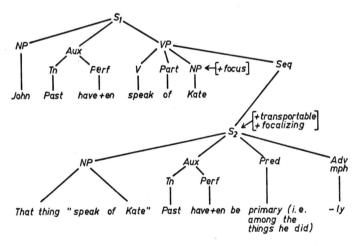

Fig. 22. The deep structure of *John had primarily spoken of Kate.*

3.4. Modification + Sequence-signalling + Focalization (Class 4)

Modifiers which also serve as sequence-signals and focalizers combine the features of Classes 2 and 3. An example of this class is the preverb *also* in

53

the following context: "Jack has influenza. John is also ill." In fig. 23, which in the form of a generalized phrase-marker shows the relationship between these two sentences, a lexicalist position has been adopted as regards the generation of *also*. The symbol # in a ring is used in the same way as in fig. 20, i.e. as an intonation morpheme that indicates where the surface structure sentences will end.

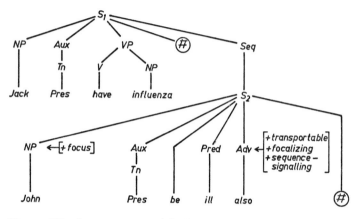

Fig. 23. The deep structure of *Jack has influenza. John is also ill.*

If *also* were to be derived transformationally, the category Seq would have to be substituted for Adv in S_2. Then Adv would be rewritten as S_3, which in simplified form would run as "That thing 'John is ill' is all so as that thing 'Jack has influenza'", where *all* has the meaning "entirely" or "completely". This transformational derivation has, however, the drawback that it preserves an original notion of manner that is no longer existent in present-day English, where *also* denotes pure addition. The disappearance of the notion of manner has been accompanied by a corresponding weakening of the stress of *so* in *also*. Another preverb denoting addition that similarly has lost at least most of its original notion of manner is the preverb *likewise*, which can be substituted for *also* in the example discussed: "Jack has influenza. John is likewise ill."[23]

Attaching the features [+focus] and [focalizing] to the elements *John* and *also* in order to indicate their functional relationship seems to be a somewhat

---

[23] The observant reader may have noticed that in the sentence beginning "Another preverb denoting addition that similarly has lost at least most of its original notion of manner" there is still another synonym of *also*, namely *similarly*, which in this context denotes both addition and manner. For further examples see Jacobson 1964: 26.

54

simpler method than that which I used in Jacobson 1968*a*, where in a discussion of a similar three-function case I advocated the addition of a special deletable function-phrase to the generalized phrase-marker.[24]

3.5. *Pure Focalization*

Pure focalization may be exemplified by *only* in such a sentence as *John, only, has mentioned Kate* (= *Only John has mentioned Kate*). As appears from fig. 24, which is an attempt to render the deep structure of this sentence, there is in this case no preverbial modification, as *only* is an NP-operator, and the definition of preverbial modifier given in 3.1 only includes categories dominating strings containing a verb (cf. Jacobson 1966: 117).

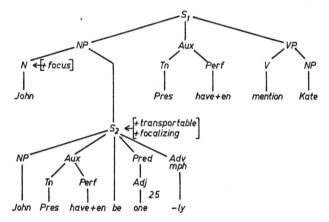

Fig. 24. The deep structure of *John, only, has mentioned Kate.*

Instead of deriving *only* from a sentence (S₂), as in fig. 24, it might be preferable to insert it directly as a lexical item with such features as [+transportable] and [+focalizing]. In that case base rules must be formulated in such a way that the optional S dominated by an NP can be replaced by an Adv with the feature [+focalizing].

---

[24] When I was writing Jacobson 1968*a*, Chomsky had not yet introduced the system of attaching features to non-lexical categories in phrase-markers (cf. 1.1, par. 5).

[25] *One* is here used in the same sense as the adjective *only*. This sense may be found in such contexts as *She is the one person who can do it*. Instead of inserting this adjective *one* under Pred we could of course insert the adjective *only* and let it be followed by a zero adverb morpheme. It is worth noting that *alone* can be substituted for *only* in the postnominal position: *John alone has mentioned Kate.* This adverb may in a similar way be derived from the adjective *alone* (= all, i.e. completely, one) + a zero adverb morpheme.

3.6. *Focalization + Sequence-signalling*

A combination of focalization and sequence-signalling may be found in the word *also* if we change fig. 23 in such a way that *also* is treated not as an S-operator but as an NP-operator, like *only* in fig. 24. The NP of S_2 in fig. 23 would then assume the configuration of fig. 25, if we allow this NP to dominate an Adv with the feature [+focalizing] (cf. 3.5, par. 2). Other features of this Adv would be [+sequence-signalling] and [+transportable], though the second one has to be queried, as many educated English-speaking people would hesitate to accept such a sentence as *Also John is ill* (with plus juncture, i.e. no pause, between *also* and *John*). Cf. Jacobson 1964: 226, n. 1.

Fig. 25. The deep structure of the noun phrase *John also* in *Jack has influenza. John also is ill.* Cf. fig. 23.

Instead of treating *also* in the sentence *John also is ill* as an NP-operator, one might alternatively treat it as a preverb in M2 (cf. fig. 9a). However, the junctural pattern, which makes *John* and *also* into a unit in relation to the rest of the sentence, seems to speak in favour of the approach adopted in fig. 25.

4. Preverbial Meanings

Semantically preverbs can be divided into a large number of classes and sub-classes with many instances of overlap. For example, we have the classes of time and manner with their various shades of meaning, but we also find pre-verbs which denote both manner and time in the same sentence. Such semantic mixture may vary in strength in different acts of performance. If we want to obtain a rough estimate of the mode, i.e. the most frequent type, and the range of this mixture, we may use a cline on which the individual cases can be set off. Fig. 26 is an attempt to illustrate such a semantic cline graphically. In this figure the vertical axis denotes manner and the horizontal axis time. If in a sentence a preverb like *regularly* can be said to mean *in a regular manner* with no temporal sense at all, then it is set off at A. If on the other hand it is synonymous with *constantly* or *always*, i.e. is purely temporal, it is set off at C. All other occurrences where the senses of manner and time are mixed in varying degrees are set off at corresponding points between A and C. For example, B denotes the position of an occurrence where the semantic content of *regularly* is a mixture of manner and time, with the manner component somewhat stronger than the time component.

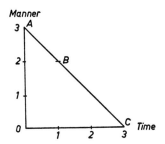

Fig. 26. Graph illustrating a semantic cline.

Dictionaries vary a great deal in accuracy and taxonomic delicacy as regards the rendering of such pure and mixed senses. Thus NID_3 gives to *regularly* only the sense "in a regular, orderly, lawful, or methodical way". Wyld, in his *Universal English Dictionary*, on the other hand, is aware both of the pure senses of manner and time and their mixture. This he shows by explaining the meaning of *regularly* by such synonymous expressions as "in a regular manner" (pure manner), "at regular intervals or periods" (mixture of manner and time), and "constantly" (pure time).

Hallander (1966: 18–19) accounts for similar types of polysemy by speaking of semantic components which together make up the full content of a word. In the individual occurrences one or more components may then very well be non-present or one particular component may dominate over the others.

In transformational grammar the meaning, or in the case of polysemy the various semantic components, of a preverb can be denoted in phrase-markers by means of semantic features such as [+descriptive] for manner and [+temporal] for time. These features have also a syntactic function by playing a part in determining whether a preverb should be S- or VP-operating and consequently how it should be placed. Chomsky (1965: 79 ff.) ascribes to nouns such syntactic features as [+abstract] and [+human], but as far as adverbials are concerned he regards Place, Time, Manner, etc. as categories on the same level as S, NP, Adj, etc. (see, for example, Chomsky 1965: 102). It seems, however, to be more logical to speak of Adverbials on the categorial level and then distinguish them in the subcategorization process by means of such features as [+locative], [+temporal], [+descriptive], etc. This makes it possible to denote a mixture of two or more semantic components in the way indicated by fig. 27, where a combination of the following two meaning contents is intended:

(*a*) Nevertheless John could rejoice (contrast).
(*b*) John could continue to rejoice (time).

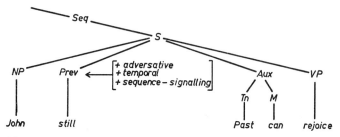

Fig. 27. The deep structure of *John still could rejoice.*

The relative strength of the two semantic components is denoted in fig. 27 only by means of the order in which the features are enumerated, as it is difficult to emulate the delicacy of the semantic cline within the framework of a phrase-marker. On the other hand, one can include more than two components, which is not possible in a cline of the simple type illustrated in fig. 26.[26] The value of denoting the relative strength of the various semantic components is especially evident if we want to translate a sentence like *John still could rejoice* into a language that does not mix time and contrast in the same word, e.g. German, which must use either the word *noch* (pure time) or the word *doch* (pure contrast). In such cases we must disregard the weaker component in favour of the stronger one.

Syntactic and semantic features can very well co-occur. Thus in fig. 27 the syntactic feature [+sequence-signalling] has been added to the two semantic features. In this way the close relationship between these different types of features in giving a preverb its full contextual content is clearly indicated.[27]

---

[26] For a diagram illustrating more complex semantic compositions, see Hallander 1966: 19.
[27] Cf. Jacobson 1964: 42 ff., where several examples of the relationship between meaning and function are given.

5. Auxiliary Transformations in English

1. Introductory: Phrase Structure Rules

The present treatment of auxiliary transformations will be based on the following four phrase structure rules.

(1) *PS rule 1*[1]

	Abbreviations
S →NP+VP (S) (Seq)	Seq = sequence sentence
Seq→(Coord) S	Coord = coordinator

With Lyons (1968: 333) I envisage the possibility of a base component with universal deep structure categories such as NP and VP, which in their turn are associated with language-dependent features of various kinds. An English NP, then, has grammatical features denoting number, definiteness, and generic category (cf. Bach 1967: 464). Similarly, an English VP has grammatical features denoting tense, number agreement, mood, and aspect. In the rules and diagrams of the present book all these features will not be explicitly marked. Thus in the case of VP only certain tense, aspect, and number agreement features will be given, namely

Tense: [−tn][2] in sentences with no special tense and [+tn] in others. The latter is further specified by the features [+pres] or [+past] for the present and past tenses. If [+past] is not realized as the morpheme [ed],[2] the feature [+strong] to denote strong conjugation is also added.

Aspect: [+perf] and [+prog] for the perfective and progressive aspects.

Number: [+sing] and [+plur] for singular and plural number, if the tense feature is [+pres].

This feature representation replaces part of the earlier Aux formula, which ran as follows (for instance, Chomsky 1965: 43 and Thomas 1966: 130):

(2) Aux→Tense (Modal) (*have*+*en*) (*be*+*ing*)[3]

---

[1] Note that rules and examples are numbered serially within brackets.
[2] Features and their realizations as words or morphemes in the terminal string are given within square brackets.
[3] Optional constituents are given within round brackets.

Lakoff (1965: A-3 ff.) seems to be the first transformationalist to dispense with the constituent Aux in the deep structure by treating tenses as grammatical features of verbs and adjectives. Other work, for example by Grady (1967), Bach (1967), Ross (1967*b*), and Ellegård (in preparation), has given convincing proof that it is preferable to assume that the modals, the perfect tenses, and the progressive forms are generated by T rules instead of by PS rules.[4]

The symbol Seq in (1) denotes an optional sequence sentence. Most utterances consist of a sequence of sentences, and this symbol can be used to connect these to each other, thus serving the purpose of extending the range of transformational grammar to the utterance level and other suprasentential levels. A sequence sentence can also be transformed into an adverbial. The optional coordinator, e.g. *but, and, or*,[5] is outside the domination of the following S-node. Sequence-signalling constituents, e.g. *he* and *in that way*, on the other hand, are dominated by this S-node (fig. 1).

---

[4] Grady reacts against the possibility of generating such sentences as **I may have been being a good cook* from the earlier Aux formula when it is followed by *be* + Pred. He therefore removes (*be* + *ing*) from Aux and instead treats *ing* as a nominalizer of the main verb, so that V + *ing* can be placed in the Pred position of *be* + Pred.

Bach eliminates the forms *have* and *be* in their use both as main verbs and as auxiliaries from the base and reintroduces them by transformational rules. He also shows that the resulting base rules are more in line with what he describes as a reasonable set of universal base rules than those used in earlier analyses.

Ross claims that all auxiliaries are really main verbs, and Ellegård argues that there are no hard and fast lines between modals and such main verbs as are followed by other verbs in surface structure, e.g. *want, dare*; as we have to assume sentence transformation in the latter case, consistency requires that we should do so also in the case of the modals.

[5] Some transformationalists, e.g. Ross (1967*a*: 91), propose that the conjoining of sentences with *and* and *or* be based on a rule schema of the type $S \rightarrow \left\{ {and \atop or} \right\} S^n$, where $n \geqslant 2$, i.e. a given number (n) of sentences (at least two) are generated and then conjoined. *But* is not included in the rule schema, probably because contrast requires ordering. It is, however, not only in the case of *but* that the ordering of sentences is significant, but sometimes also in the case of *and* and *or*, as in the sequence *John died, Dick disappeared, and Eric began to feel very lonely*. Here it is obvious that at least sentence no. 3 could hardly be differently placed. In such cases of *and* and *or* conjunction, a rule like PS rule 1, in my opinion, ought to be used instead of the proposed rule schema. For a discussion of cases where *and* is symmetric as opposed to cases where it means "and subsequently" or "and in consequence", see Staal 1968, and for a brief note on the rule schema, see McCawley 1968*a*: fn. 2.

To sum up, then, the rule schema is suitable for such cases of conjunction with *and* and *or* as require no special ordering; otherwise a rule like PS rule 1 ought to be used. This rule is recursive, i.e. it can be applied repeatedly, and thus can be used for multiple conjunction just like the rule schema. Conjunction with *but* always requires ordering, which means that the rule schema cannot be applied.

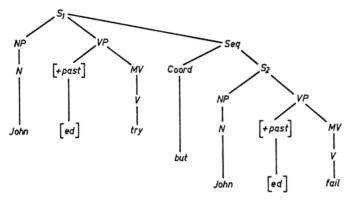

Fig. 1. The deep structure of *John tried, but he failed.*

(3) *PS rule 2*

$$NP \rightarrow \begin{Bmatrix} N \\ NP + S \end{Bmatrix}$$

In accordance with what was said above under PS rule 1 (with which compare Bach 1967: 472 and McCawley 1968a: fn. 2 and the literature there referred to), the earlier Det, i.e. determiner constituent, has been replaced by features, and NP as an alternative of being rewritten as N, is expanded with an S from which relative clauses and other NP-modifiers (including adverbials) can be derived. This expanded NP can of course in its turn be rewritten as N, so that we obtain a third alternative where NP dominates N+S.

(4) *PS rule 3*
VP → MV (S)

(5) *Ps rule 4*

$$MV \rightarrow \begin{Bmatrix} VB \\ Pred \end{Bmatrix} (S)$$

$$VB \rightarrow V \begin{Bmatrix} (NP)\ (NP) \\ (Pred) \end{Bmatrix}$$

$$Pred \rightarrow \begin{Bmatrix} Adj \\ NP \end{Bmatrix}$$

Abbreviations

VB = verbal
Pred = predicative

When MV, i.e. the main-verb phrase, is rewritten, there is first a choice between VB and Pred. If VB is selected, there is, when VB is rewritten as

V, a further choice between several optional constituents. One or two NP's are selected if V is transitive, Pred if it is a copula, e.g. *become*, and neither NP (or NP's) nor Pred if it is intransitive.[6] Two NP's occur in the generation of such surface structures as *Jack gave John money* and *John reminded me of the incident*. In the latter sentence the unstressed particle *of* originates as a feature of the verb.

2. Transformational Rules Generating or Affecting Aux

The following transformational rules generating or affecting the category Aux will be dealt with in the order in which they have to be applied to change base phrase-markers generated by PS rules 1–4 into derived phrase-markers, namely:[7]

(6)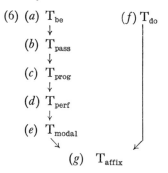

(a) T_{be} (f) T_{do}

(b) T_{pass}

(c) T_{prog}

(d) T_{perf}

(e) T_{modal}

(g) T_{affix}

The arrows denote the order of the transformations.

Transformations (b), (c), and (d) presuppose (a), and (f) is parallel with (a)–(e).

In the analyses of pre-T and post-T structure (i.e. the structure before and after the particular transformation described), the variables X, Y, and Z denote any string including a null string (as regards constraints on their use see Ross 1967a: 3 ff.)

(7) *T rule 1:* T_{be} (obligatory)

Pre-T

structure: X, NP, [+tn], Pred, Y

————— 1 2   3   4   5

<hr />

[6] For a discussion on transitivity, object-deletion, the notion pseudo-intransitive, etc., see Lyons 1968: 350 ff.
[7] The transformational cycle begins with the most deeply embedded sentences. Cf. Chomsky 1965: 134–35.

Structural

change: To 3 is attached the complex symbol [*be*, +Aux], where *be* stands
            for a feature matrix of the usual sort and [+Aux] denotes the
            derived, i.e. transformationally introduced, syntactic category
            Aux that immediately dominates it in phrase-markers (cf.
            Chomsky 1967: 44). By the attachment 3 also becomes imme-
            diately dominated by this Aux (which in its turn is immediately
            dominated by VP).

Post-T

structure: X, NP, $_{Aux}$[+tn, be],[8] Pred, Y
            1   2   3   4   5

   If the tense feature is [−tn], this transformation does not take place; this
is the case in the generation of adverbials, for example, of the surface structure *The tree in the garden* as opposed to *The tree is in the garden*. These
sentences are based on the following terminal deep-structure strings:

The tree in the garden: [*The*] *tree* # [*the*] *tree* [−tn] [*in*] [*the*] *garden* #
                            (where the first occurrence of [*the*] *tree* erases the
                            second).[9]

The tree is in the garden: [*The*] *tree* [+tn] [*in*] [*the*] *garden*

   For phrase-marker illustrations of T$_{be}$ see figs. 2 and 3.

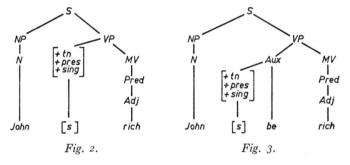

Fig. 2.   Fig. 3.

Fig. 2. The deep structure of *John is rich.*

Fig. 3. Intermediate structure of *John is rich* after T$_{be}$.

---

[8] This means that Aux immediately dominates what is enclosed in the square brackets.
Cf. Chomsky 1967.

[9] # = sentence boundary.

(8) *T-rule 2:* T_{pass} (obligatory)

(*a*) Passive with an agent

Pre-T

structure: X, NP, $_{Aux}$[+tn, be], [it] # NP, [en], V, NP, [+ag],[10] NP, Y # Z

       1 2   3   4 5 6   7 8 9   10   11 12 13 14

where 2=9, and 6=11;

where 4 is a realization of a noun with the feature [+pro];

and where 7 is a generalized realization of the V feature (+pass).

(Only verbs with this feature can be passivized. See Svartvik 1967 and cf. Chomsky 1967: 27).

Structural

changes: 2 erases 9, and 11 erases 6;

4 undergoes *it*-deletion (Ross 1967*a*: 102);

5 and 13 ⇒ null.

Post-T

structure: X, NP, $_{Aux}$[+tn, be], [en], V, [+ag], NP, Y, Z

       1 2   3   7 8   10 11 12 14

10 and 11 (=the agent phrase) are assumed to be the result of a transformation.

For phrase-marker illustrations of T_{pass} with an agent see figs. 4 and 5.

(*b*) Agentless passive (actional or statal)

Pre-T

structure: X, NP, $_{Aux}$[+tn, be], [it] # [someone], [en], V, NP, Y # Z

        1 2   3   4 5   6   7 8 9 10 11 12

where 2=9;

where 4 is a realization of a noun with the feature [+pro];

where 6 is a realization of a noun with the features [+pro, −def];

and where 7 is a generalized realization of either the V feature [+pass] alone (=actional passive) or a combination of [+pass] and the VP feature [+perf] (=statal passive).

[10] As Svartvik points out (1966: 30–31), *by* is not the only preposition that can introduce a phrase with an agentive function in a passive sentence. Therefore 10 is given not as the specific feature realization [*by*] but as the more general agent feature [+ag]. *By* is, however, the only preposition that merely requires the preceding verb to have the feature [+pass], and no other selectional restrictions are involved, as in the case of prepositions which are specially selected by their respective verbs, e.g. *in* after *interested* and *about* after *worried*. Svartvik (1966: 102) calls these quasi-agents and points out that they are cases of collocation as opposed to *by*-agents which are cases of colligation.

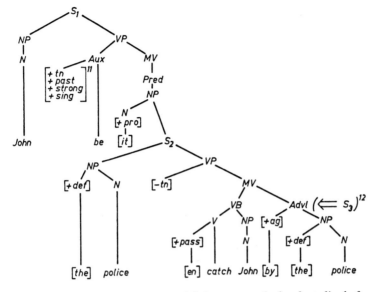

Fig. 4. Intermediate structure of *John was caught by the police* before T_{pass}. Advl = adverbial.

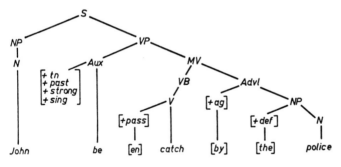

Fig. 5. Intermediate structure of *John was caught by the police* after T_{pass}.

Structural
changes: 2 erases 9;
           4 undergoes *it*-deletion;
           5, 6, and 13 ⇒ null.

___

[11] The feature [+strong] denotes that *be* undergoes strong conjugation in the past tense.

[12] The terminal string of S_3 would run as follows in the deep structure:
[The] catch [ing] [−tn] [by] [the] police.

Post-T

structure: X, NP, $_{Aux}$[+tn, be], [en], V, Y, Z

    I 2 3   7 8 10 12

For phrase-marker illustrations see figs. 6 and 7, (a) and (b). As the phrase-markers showing pre-T structure in the (a) figures are identical with the phrase-marker in fig. 4, except in the case of S_2, only S_2 is diagrammed in these figures.

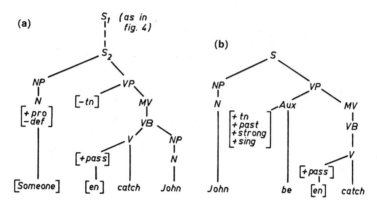

Fig. 6. Intermediate structure of *John was caught* (actional passive with the meaning *John got caught*) before T_{pass} (a) and after T_{pass} (b).

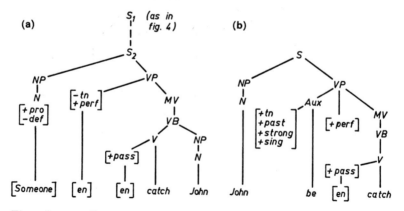

Fig. 7. Intermediate structure of *John was caught* (statal passive with the meaning *John had been caught*) before erasure of the first of the two identical [en] and before T_{pass} (a), and after T_{pass} (b).

66

(9) *T rule 3:* T_{prog} (obligatory)

Pre-T
structure: X, NP, $_{Aux}$[+tn, be], [it] # NP, [ing], V, Y # Z

             1 2   3   4 5 6   7 8 9 10 11

         where 2 = 6;

         where 4 is a realization of a noun with the feature [+pro];

         where 7 is a realization of the VP feature [+prog];[13]

         and where 8 can alternatively be *be*, so that a structure that has
         undergone T_{be} alone or T_{be} followed by T_{pass} can also undergo
         T_{prog}. (In this case the free variable 9 denotes MV. See figs. 3, 5,
         6*b*, 7*b*).

Structural
changes: 2 erases 6;

          4 undergoes *it*-deletion;

          5 and 10 ⇒ null.

Post-T
structure: X, NP, $_{Aux}$[+tn, be], [ing], V, Y, Z

            1 2   3   7 8 9 11

For phrase-marker illustrations see fig. 8, (*a*) and (*b*).

The development of the terminal string in cases where T_{prog} is applied to
a structure that has undergone T_{pass} or T_{be} is exemplified in (10), where
⌢ denotes morphemic adherence.

(10) (a) *Intermediate structure*

$T_{be} + T_{prog}$ {(i) After T_{be}: John [s]⌢be [a] fool
            {(ii) After T_{prog}: John [s]⌢be [ing]⌢be [a] fool

$T_{pass} + T_{prog}$ {(iii) *After* T_{pass}: [The] house [s]⌢be [en]⌢paint
            {(iv) *After* T_{prog}: [The] house [s]⌢be [ing]⌢be [en]⌢paint

   (b) *Surface structure*

(i) John is a fool.   (iii) The house is painted.

(ii) John is being a fool.   (iv) The house is being painted.

---

[13] This feature belongs to the phrase-structure subcomponent of the base. The features [+nounal] and [+adjectival], which most probably belong to the lexicon, often also have the realization [ing] when they change a verb into a noun or adjective. Thus the feature [+nounal] can turn a verb like *paint* into the noun *painting* (with an abstract or concrete meaning depending on whether it has the further feature [+abstract] or [−abstract]) and the feature [+adjectival] can turn a verb like *interest* into the adjective *interesting*.

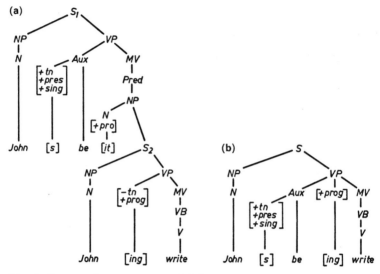

Fig. 8. Intermediate structure of *John is writing* before T_{prog} (*a*) and after T_{prog} (*b*).

(11) *T rule 4:* T_{perf} (obligatory)

Pre-T

structure: X, NP, $_{Aux}[+tn, have]$, [it] $\#$ NP, [en], V, Y $\#$ Z

1 2 3 4 5 6 7 8 9 10 11

where 2 = 6;

where *have* in 3 is derived from *be* [*by*] by means of a *have*-transformation (T_{have}), which in its turn is caused by an ergative transformation ($T_{ergative}$);[14] (for the pre-T structure of these two transformations see fig. 9);

where 4 is a realization of a noun with the feature [+pro];

where 7 is a generalized realization of the VP feature [+perf];

and where 8 can alternatively be *be* so that T_{perf} can apply to structures which have already undergone T_{be} alone, or T_{be} followed by T_{pass} and/or T_{prog} (the free variable 9 adapts its content accordingly).

Structural

changes: 2 erases 6;

4 undergoes *it*-deletion;

5 and 10 ⇒ null.

---

[14] Cf. Lyons 1968: 351–52 and 395–97.

Post-T
structure: X, NP, $_{Aux}$[+tn, have], [en], V, Y, Z
           1   2   3   7 8 9 11

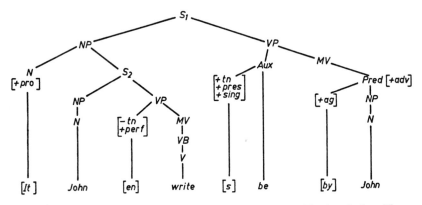

Fig. 9. Intermediate structure of *John has written* after T_{be} but before T_{have}, which changes the string *be* [by][15] into *have*, and also before $T_{ergative}$, which makes the NP of S_1 and the NP of Pred change places.

For phrase-marker illustrations of T_{perf} see fig. 10, (*a*) and (*b*).

If T_{perf} is applied to example (10) (*a*) (i), which has already undergone T_{be}, the result in intermediate structure will be

(12) John [s]⌃have [en]⌃be [a] fool

which gives the surface structure *John has been a fool.*

Similarly, if T_{perf} is applied to example (10) (*a*) (iv), which has already undergone T_{pass} and T_{prog}, the result in intermediate structure will be

(13) [The] house [s]⌃have [en]⌃be [ing]⌃be [en]⌃paint

which gives the surface structure *The house has been being painted.*

---

[15] In other cases of $T_{ergative}$, e.g. in the generation of possessive *have*, various other features and prepositions occur. Thus the post T_{be} string [*A*] *hat* [s] *be* [*with*] [*the*] *man* is changed by $T_{ergative}$ into [*The*] *man* [s] *have* [*a*] *hat*, which gives the surface structure *The man has a hat.* If, however, the tense feature in the deep structure is [− tn], no T_{be} takes place and accordingly no T_{have} either, so that the preposition *with* remains. In this way we obtain the surface structure *The man with a hat*, if the deep structure [*A*] *hat* [− tn] [*with*] [*the*] *man* is the S of an expanded NP whose N is [*the*] *man*. The change from the deep structure *The man* #[*a*] *hat* [− tn] [*with*] [*the*] *man*# into the surface structure *The man with a hat* involves first $T_{ergative}$ and then deletion of the second redundant occurrence of [*the*] *man*. Cf. Fillmore 1966: 25 and 30 and Bach 1967: 466.

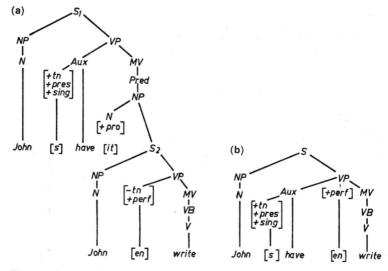

Fig. 10. Intermediate structure of *John has written* before T_{perf} (*a*) and after T_{perf} (*b*).

(14) T rule 5: T_{modal} (obligatory)
(a) Transitive modal

Pre-T
structure:

    X, NP, [+tn], V, [it] # NP, V, Y # Z

    1 2   3   4 5 6 7   8 9 10 11

    where 2=7;

    where 4, besides [+V], has the feature [+modal] and belongs
    to a closed group comprising the following verbs: *shall* (*should*),
    will (*would*), *can* (*could*), *may* (*might*), and *must*; to these may be
    added *need* and *dare* when they follow the same pattern;[16]
    where 5 is a realization of a noun with the feature [+pro];
    and where 8 can alternatively be *be* or *have* so that T_{modal} can
    apply to structures which have already undergone T_{be} alone, or
    T_{be} followed by T_{pass} and/or T_{prog} and/or T_{perf} (the free variable
    9 adapts its content accordingly).

Structural
changes: 2 erases 7;

    4 is attached to 3 and its category feature [+V] is replaced by

---

[16] Cf. Svartvik 1966: 15 ("class *a'1*") and Thomas 1966: 129.

[+Aux]; by this attachment and substitution both 3 and 4 become immediately dominated by the derived syntactic category Aux (which in its turn is immediately dominated by VP); cf. (7).

5 undergoes *it*-deletion;

6 and 10 ⇒ null.

Post-T
structure: X, NP, $_{Aux}$[+tn, +modal], V, Y, Z
1   2   3   4   8 9 11

For phrase-marker illustrations of T_{modal} with a transitive modal see fig. 11 *a* and *b*.

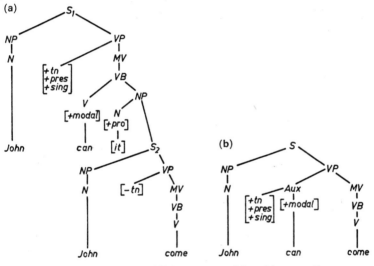

Fig. *11*. The deep structure of *John can come* (*a*) and intermediate structure of the same sentence after T_{modal} (*b*).

(b) Intransitive modal

Pre-T
structure: X, [it] # NP, [−tn], V, Y # [+tn], V, Z
1   2   3   4   5   6 7 8   9   10 11
where 2 is a realization of a noun with the feature [+pro];
where 6 can alternatively be *be* or *have* (see (14*a*);
and where 10, besides [+V], has the feature [+modal] (see (14*a*)).

Structural
changes: 2 undergoes *it*-deletion;

3 and 8 ⇒ null;

10 is attached to 9 and its category feature [+V] is replaced by [+Aux]; by this attachment and substitution both 9 and 10 become immediately dominated by the derived syntactic category Aux; this node then replaces 5 and thus comes to be immediately dominated by the VP dominating 5.

Post-T
structure: X, NP $_{Aux}$[+tn, +modal], V, Y, Z
      1   4   5   9   10   6 7 11

For phrase-marker illustrations of T_{modal} with an intransitive modal see fig. 12, (*a*) and (*b*), and for more examples of the two types of modal see Ross 1967*b*: 11–13.

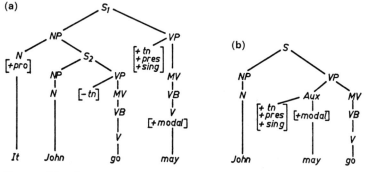

Fig. 12. The deep structure of *John may go* in the sense *John will perhaps go* (*a*) and intermediate structure of the same sentence after T_{modal} (*b*). (*John may go* in the sense *John is allowed to go* has a deep structure similar to that of fig. 11*a*.)

(15) The following examples show the development of the terminal string in cases where T_{modal} is applied to structures which have already undergone T_{be} alone, or T_{be} followed by T_{pass} and/or T_{prog} and/or T_{perf}.

(a) *Intermediate structure*

$T_{be}+T_{modal}$ { (i) *After* T_{be}: John [s]⌢be [a] fool
(ii) *After* T_{modal}: John must be [a] fool

$T_{pass}+T_{modal}$ { (iii) *After* T_{pass}: [The] house [s]⌢be [en]⌢paint
(iv) After T_{modal}: [The] house must be [en]⌢paint

72

$T_{prog} + T_{modal}$ $\begin{cases}\text{(v) } \textit{After } T_{prog}\text{: John [s]\^be [ing]\^come} \\ \text{(vi) } \textit{After } T_{modal}\text{: John will be [ing]\^come}\end{cases}$

$T_{perf} + T_{modal}$ $\begin{cases}\text{(vii) } \textit{After } T_{perf}\text{: John [s]\^have [en]\^write} \\ \text{(viii) } \textit{After } T_{modal}\text{: John must have [en]\^write}\end{cases}$

$T_{pass} + T_{prog}$ $+ T_{perf} + T_{modal}$ $\begin{cases}\text{(ix) } \textit{After } T_{pass} + T_{prog} + T_{perf}\text{: See (13)} \\ \text{(x) } \textit{After } T_{modal}\text{: [The] house must have [en]\^be} \\ \qquad\qquad\qquad\quad \text{[ing]\^be [en]\^paint}\end{cases}$

(b) *Surface structure*

(i) John is a fool.   (v) John is coming.
(ii) John must be a fool.   (vi) John will be coming.
(iii) The house is painted   (vii) John has written.
(iv) The house must be painted   (viii) John must have written.
(ix) The house has been being painted.
(x) The house must have been being painted.

(16) *T rule 6:* $T_{do \text{ (emph and/or neg)}}$ (obligatory)[17]

Pre-T
structure: X, NP, [+tn], [+emph], [+neg], V, it # NP, V, Y # Z
               1 2   3   4   5   6 7 8 9   10 11 12 13
            where 2 = 9;
            where 3, 4, and 5 are VP features; of these 4 or 5 can optionally
            be omitted; 4 is realized in the phonological component as
            emphatic stress and intonation, and 5 is realized as *not* (which,
            just like certain auxiliary forms, can undergo contraction);
            where 6, besides [+V], has the feature [+pro] (this feature com-
            bination only applies to the verb *do*);[18]
            and where 7 is a realization of a noun with the feature [+pro].

Structural
changes: 2 erases 9;
            6 is attached to 3, and its category feature [+V] is replaced by
            [+Aux]; by this attachment and substitution both 3 and 6 be-
            come immediately dominated by the derived syntactic category

---

[17] Abbreviations: emph = emphasis; neg = negative.
[18] Apart from being auxiliarized by T_{do}, the pro-verb *do* is used in such contexts as:
He has not acted as he should have done (Curme 1931: 22).

Aux (which in its turn is immediately dominated by VP); cf. (7) and (14);

7 undergoes *it*-deletion;

8 and 12 ⇒ null

Post-T

structure: X, NP, $_{Aux}$[+tn, do], [+emph], [+neg], V, Y, Z

       1   2   3   6   4   5   10 11 13

It should be noted that in the pre-T structure term no. 10 cannot be replaced by Aux, i.e. T_{do} does not apply to the auxiliaries *be, have, can, will*, etc.[19] Nor can any auxiliarization transformation (including T_{do} itself) apply to *do* once it has been auxiliarized. It is for this reason that T_{do} is described in (6) as parallel with all other auxiliarization transformations.

For phrase-marker illustrations of T_{do} see fig. 13, (*a*) and (*b*).

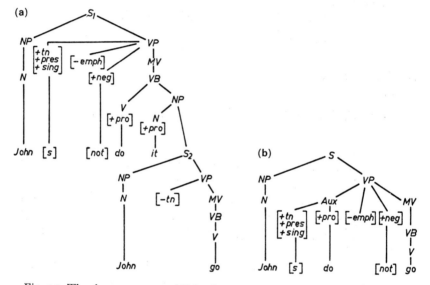

Fig. 13. The deep structure of *John does not go* (*a*) and intermediate structure of the same sentence after $T_{do\ (neg)}$ (*b*).

Another type of T_{do} is $T_{do\ (interrogative)}$, which applies to a structure where the subject NP and the VP feature [+tn] have changed places because of a

---

[19] In the imperative *Do(n't) be kind*, which looks like an exception, the pro-verb *do* has been auxiliarized in a way differing from T_{do}: it substitutes for the auxiliary *will*. See Klima 1964: 257 ff.

question transformation. In this case both the features [+emph] and [+neg] are optional, not only one of them as in the transformation described above.

The reason for the application of T_{do}, irrespective of type, is explained by Klima (1964: 256–57) as the necessity to have direct contact between [+tn] and a following V or Aux because otherwise T_{affix} cannot apply. In a sentence without Aux, T_{do} is therefore applied if the contiguity of [+tn] and V is blocked by [+emph] and/or [+neg].[20] Similarly in an Aux-less interrogative sentence T_{do} is applied if the subject NP blocks the way.

(17) *T rule 7:* T_{affix} (obligatory)

Pre-T
structure: X, Af, v, Y

            1 2 3 4

where 2 stands for the feature realizations [s] and [ed] from [+tn], [en] from [+pass] or [+perf], and [ing] from [+prog];

and where 3 can be either V or one of the auxiliaries *be, have, do, can, may*, etc. (see T rules 1–6).

Structural
change: 2 becomes a suffix of 3.

Post-T
structure: X, v+Af, Y

            1 3 2 4

Later rules take care of irregularities, so that when, for example, the terminal string of fig. 3 has been transformed by T_{affix} from *John* [s] *be rich* into *John be+s rich*, the auxiliary *be+s* finally becomes *is* in the surface structure. For further illustration compare the intermediate structures and the surface structures in (15).

Against the inclusion of T_{affix} in the grammar, it may be argued that if the features enumerated in the first *where*-clause under Pre-T structure above had been placed after their respective verbs or auxiliaries from the beginning, no changing of places in the case of terms no. 2 and 3 would have been necessary and that this would have simplified the grammar. The features have, however, been made to precede their respective verbs or auxiliaries for the following two reasons:

---

[20] [−emph] and [−neg], on the other hand, have no influence, as redundancy rules will delete them before the application of T_{do}.

(1) The contiguity between V and a following VP feature may be blocked by an optional S branching out from MV or an optional NP or Pred branching out from VB (see (5)), and this would have necessitated a complicated permutation transformation to ensure contiguity before affixation.[21]

(2) T_{do} would have to be given a more complicated form if it could not be based on the rule that it occurs if [+emph] and/or [+neg], or, in the case of $T_{do\ (interrogative)}$, the subject NP, block the way between [+tn] and V.

---

[21] Fig. 5 in paper no. 6 shows the blocking performed by an NP ("the plan") branching out from VB.

6. Various Types of Adverbialization

Introduction

The discussion on the generation of adverbials in this paper is based on the same phrase-structure rules and feature system as in paper no. 5. Most of the features are denoted in phrase-markers as segments that branch out from the constituents to which the features belong. According to Jacobs and Rosenbaum 1968: ch. 14, such branching segmentation is caused by transformations. It seems, however, that the branching can equally well be assumed to take place in the base during the application of the subcategorization rules that add features to the constituents generated by the PS rules. These rules, then, may be thought of as being of two types: subscript rules and branching rules. The first type, which simply adds features as subscripts to constituents, may be exemplified by (1) (i) and (ii).

(1) (i) $VP \rightarrow VP$
$[-tn]$

(ii) $N \rightarrow N$
$$\begin{bmatrix} horse \\ +N \\ +common \\ +concrete \\ +animate \\ -human \\ +count \end{bmatrix}$$

where *horse* represents a phonological feature matrix.

The second type which produces branching feature segments only applies to certain features, e.g. the VP feature $[+tn]$, which is added by rule (2).

(2) $VP \rightarrow [+tn] \ MV \ (S)$

This rule, which is based on PS rule 3 of paper no. 5, states that $[+tn]$ should be attached to a sister branch preceding the constituents that branch out from VP. For a phrase-marker illustration of the two rules see, for example, fig. 1. Certain features have to be duplicated. Thus if $[+sing]$ categorizes the NP immediately dominated by S (i.e. the subject NP), the VP must have the same feature unless its tense feature is [−tn].

This assignment of branching feature segmentation to the base is not the only respect in which my treatment of features differs from that of Jacobs and Rosenbaum 1968. According to them features occur at the bottom of a base phrase-marker and are moved to higher levels only by transformations. I have instead followed a suggestion by Lyons 1968: 333 that the subcategorization rules may be thought of as "associating features of tense, mood, aspect, number, definiteness, etc., *at various levels* of the constituent-structure generated by the categorial subcomponent" (i.e. the PS rules).[1]

Subcategorization rules give Pred the feature [+adv] when it is adverbial and [−adv] when it is non-adverbial. The feature [+adv] usually branches off from Pred and is then together with other more specific features such as [+manner], [+locative], or [+agent] realized as various affixes and relation-words, e.g. the *ly* that is added to adjectives and prepositions like *in* and *by* that are made to precede noun phrases.[2] If [+adv], on the other hand, is added as a subscript of Pred, we obtain affix-less adverbs or preposition-less adverbial phrases, which occur, for example, in the generation of such surface structures as

(2)　(i) He looked *hard* at me.
　　(ii) He lived *thirty years*.
　　(iii) He went *home*.
　　(iv) He knows *now*.
　　(v) He lives *here*.

The adverbs in (iii)–(v) are suitably derived from NP's; this derivation is supported by the fact that they have prepositional counterparts, e.g. *at home*, *by now*, *in here* (this *in* can also be postpositional: *herein*). In this respect they resemble the phrase *thirty years* in (ii), which can optionally take a preposition like *for* or even a "postposition" like *ago*. It is also noteworthy that such adverbs as *now* and *here* can be followed by a relative clause, e.g. *Now that you are rich* or *Here where the world is quiet*, which is another argument in favor of the assumption that they are suitably derived from NP's.

Adverbialization, i.e. the transition of an NP or Adj dominated by a Pred with the feature [+adv] into a surface structure adverbial can take place in various ways, which I will now describe.

---

[1] The italics are mine.
[2] The status of prepositions in a transformational grammar is discussed, for example, by Fillmore 1966 and by Jacobs and Rosenbaum 1968, ch. 17.

1. The Pred occurs in a sentence whose subject NP is not deleted

Three cases can here be distinguished and in all of them adverbialization takes place by means of the following transformation:[3]

(3) *T rule 1:* Simple T_{adv} (obligatory)

Pre-T
structure: X, Pred, Y
       1   2   3
       where 2 has the feature $[+adv]$.

Structural
change: 2 ⇒ Advl. If this 2 is dominated by a VP node with the feature $[-tn]$, this VP node and its dominated MV node are simultaneously deleted.

Post-T
structure: X, Advl, Y
       1   2   3

The three cases can be described on the basis of the following functional positions of Pred in the sentence.

(*a*) The Pred can be immediately dominated by an MV that in its turn is immediately dominated by a VP with the feature $[+tn]$. Then a later transformation adds *be* (see T rule 1 in paper no. 5), so that we obtain such surface structures as

(4)   (i) John is in the country.
      (ii) The meeting is on Sunday.

(*b*) The Pred can be preceded by V in immediate domination by VB (see PS rule 4).[4] Then with Lyons (1968: 346–49) we may regard V as a temporal or locative copula in such surface structures as

(5)   (i) The accident happened last week.
      (ii) These events occurred in Stockholm.

---

[3] In analyses of pre-T and post-T structure (i.e. the structure before and after the particular transformation described) such variables as X, Y, Z, and W denote any string including a null string.
[4] For the various PS rules see paper no. 5.

(c) The Pred can be preceded by a subject NP which dominates *it* + S. An example of this is the structure underlying the surface structure sentence *John works in a factory*, when this sentence is uttered in answer to the question *Where does John work?* Then the adverbial is stressed and the essential predication of the sentence is that it is in a factory that John works and not anywhere else, and this idea is reflected by a deep structure where *in a factory* is derived from the Pred of S_1 and *John works* from an S_2 embedded in the subject NP. See fig. 1.

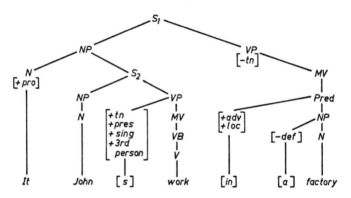

Fig. *1*. The deep structure of *John works in a factory* (in answer to the question *Where does John work?*). The VP feature [− tn] may be read out as "occurs" for easier comprehension of the structural relationships (cf. Lakoff 1967: 15). Def = definite, Loc = locative.

Note that it does not matter where the stress is strongest in the question, i.e. the answer to each of the alternatives in (6) has the deep structure of fig. 1.

(6)   (i) WHERE does John work?
      (ii) Where does JOHN work?
      (iii) Where does John WORK?

In order to turn the deep structure of fig. 1 into a surface structure the following transformations are necessary:

1. *It*-deletion (this transformation occurs whenever *it* is immediately followed by a noun phrase complement that has the form of a sentence), which causes the phrase-marker to undergo the further change that the NP and VP of S_2 replace the NP and VP nodes of S_1 (so-called tree-pruning, see Ross 1967a: 24 ff.).

2. Simple T_{adv}, for which see (3) above.

3. T_{affix}, which transposes the VP tense feature and V (see T rule 7 in paper no. 5).

If the tense feature of the VP of S_1 had been $[+tn]$ instead of $[-tn]$, a transformation known as extraposition would have taken place and brought S_2 under the immediate domination of S_1 after its VP. This transformation, which precedes *it*-deletion, would have prevented *it* from being deleted, so that the ultimate result in surface structure would have been *It is in a factory that John works*.[5] For further information about *it*-deletion and extraposition see Jacobs and Rosenbaum 1968: ch. 21.

2. The Pred occurs in a dominated sentence whose subject NP is deleted.

The dominated sentence is generated in this way:

(7) $S \rightarrow NP + VP$ (S) (Seq), where VP is given the feature $[-tn]$
$VP \rightarrow MV$ (S)
$MV \rightarrow Pred$ (S), where Pred is given the feature $[+adv]$
$Pred \rightarrow \begin{Bmatrix} NP \\ Adj \end{Bmatrix}$

The deletion of the subject NP is performed by means of the following transformation:

(8) *T rule 2*: Complex T_{adv} (obligatory)
Pre-T
structure: X, NP, VP, Y $\#$ NP, Pred $\#$ Z
              1   2   3   4 5 6   7 8 9
              where some kind of identity exists between 6 (or a sentence dominated by 6) and the whole or part of 1–4;
              where 3 can be null; and
              where the VP that dominates 7 has the feature $[-tn]$ and 7 itself has the feature $[+adv]$.

---

[5] The auxiliary *is* is here introduced by T_{be} (see T rule 1 in paper no. 5) and *that* is introduced by a clause complementizer transformation (Jacobs and Rosenbaum 1968: 164).

Structural
changes: 6 is erased by that constituent of 1–4 which is identical with it; if
            6 dominates *it* + S, *it*-deletion first occurs;
            5 and 8 ⇒ null;
            7 (together with its dominating nodes VP and MV) ⇒ Advl.

Post-T
structure:
$$\left\{\begin{array}{cccccc}
X, & NP, & VP, & Y, & Advl, & Z \\
1 & 2 & 3 & 4 & 7 & 9 \\
X, & NP, & Y, & Advl, & Z \\
1 & 2 & 4 & 7 & 9
\end{array}\right\}$$
where the braces enclose two
alternatives

Five cases can be distinguished on the basis of the origin of the initial S
in (7). Thus this S can be

(*a*) the optional S that is generated by rewriting S according to PS rule 1;
(*b*) the S into which the optional Seq of PS rule 1 is rewritten;
(*c*) the S with which NP can be expanded according to PS rule 2;
(*d*) the optional S that is generated by rewriting VP according to PS rule 3;
(*e*) the optional S that is generated by rewriting MV according to PS rule 4.

An example of case (*a*), i.e. S-operation,[6] is the generation of *fortunately* in
the sentence *John fortunately knows*, as depicted in figs. 2 and 3.

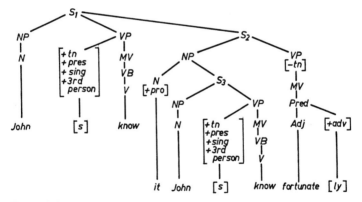

Fig. 2. The deep structure of *John fortunately knows*.

After the application of *it*-deletion and complex T_{adv} the node Advl
dominating *fortunately* is the only remaining constituent of the original S_2.

---

[6] For the terms S-operation, NP-operation, etc. see paper no. 1, section 2.

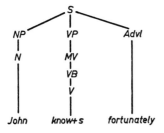

Fig. 3. The intermediate structure of *John fortunately knows* before intra-nodal transportation.

After T_{affix} Advl is moved to mid-position by a transformation which I call intra-nodal transportation. This transformation is based on the transportability convention suggested by Keyser, which "permits a particular constituent to occupy any position in a derived tree so long as the sister relationships with all other nodes in the tree are maintained" (Keyser 1968: 368). See (9).

(9) *T rule 3:* $T_{\text{intra-nodal transportation}}$ (optional)

Pre-T
structure: Ø, X, Ø, Y, Ø, Z, Ø, W, Advl
           1 2 3 4 5 6 7 8   9
           where Ø is a zero constituent;
           where 1–9 are immediately dominated by the same node; and
           where at least one of the variables X, Y, Z, and W is non-null.

Structural
changes: $\begin{Bmatrix} 1 \\ 3 \\ 5 \\ 7 \end{Bmatrix} \Rightarrow 9$

This means that one of the zero constituents is filled with the content of 9. This 9 is then deleted.

9 ⇒ null

Post-T
structure: $\begin{bmatrix} \text{Advl, X, Ø, Y, Ø, Z, Ø, W} \\ 9 \quad 2 \quad 3 \quad 4 \quad 5 \quad 6 \quad 7 \quad 8 \\ \text{Ø, X, Advl, Y, Ø, Z, Ø, W} \\ 1 \quad 2 \quad 9 \quad 4 \quad 5 \quad 6 \quad 7 \quad 8 \\ \text{Ø, X, Ø, Y, Advl, Z, Ø, W} \\ 1 \quad 2 \quad 3 \quad 4 \quad 9 \quad 6 \quad 7 \quad 8 \\ \text{Ø, X, Ø, Y, Ø, Z, Advl, W} \\ 1 \quad 2 \quad 3 \quad 4 \quad 5 \quad 6 \quad 9 \quad 8 \end{bmatrix}$

The principle of adverbialization in accordance with case (*b*) may be exemplified by the generation of the sequence-signalling adverb *then* in the S_3 of fig. 20 in paper no. 4. If the PS rules on which the present paper is based had been used in that figure, its S_3 would have had a configuration resembling that of S_2 in fig. 2 above, and its terminal string would have run as follows in intermediate structure (cf. fig. 10*b* in paper no. 5): "It # they [ed] have [en] return # then", i.e. the [−tn] feature would have made S_3 tenseless, which has no practical consequence as the only remaining constituent after complex T_{adv} is *then*. This Advl is, as appears from fig. 20 in paper no. 4, attached to a Seq node. In order to be transported to the position that it has in surface structure, namely between the tense auxiliary *had* and the main verb *returned*, it must shift its nodal adherence to VP and then undergo intranodal transportation. This combination of node-shifting and intra-nodal transportation is suitably called extra-nodal transportation. For further examples of the operations of the two types of transportation discussed here see Jacobson 1970.

Case (*c*), i.e. NP-operation, is exemplified by the surface structure *The tree in the garden*, the generation of which is discussed under T rule 1 in paper no. 5.

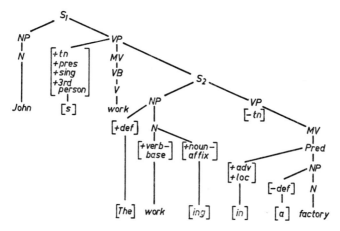

Fig. 4. The deep structure of *John works in a factory* (in answer to the question *What does John do?*). The VP feature [− tn] in S_2 may be read out as "occurs" for easier comprehension of the structural relationships.

An example of case (*d*), i.e. VP-operation, is the sentence *John works in a factory*, when it is said in answer not to the question "Where does John work?", as in 1 (c) above, but to the question "What does John do?". Then it is instead the word *work* that is stressed, and it is followed by a single-bar juncture, involving a slight pause. In this case a VP-dominated adverbial is obtained from the deep structure in fig. 4 after the application of the following transformations:

   1. Complex T_{adv}, by which the verb of S_1 erases the identical verb-base of the subject NP of S_2. The features [+def] and [+noun-affix] are also deleted as they are only determined by the context and consequently non-inherent (cf. Chomsky 1965: 182).

   2. T_{affix}, which transposes the VP tense feature and V.

   Similarly, Lakoff's example *I beat my wife in the yard* (Lakoff 1965: section F) must be assigned different deep structures according to its meaning. If the meaning is that I beat my wife in the yard and not in our house, the deep structure must be as in fig. 1. But if the sentence means that I beat, not kiss, my wife in the yard, the deep structure must be as in fig. 4.

   The fact that it is possible to have a single-bar juncture before *in a factory* in case (d) is one criterion that it is a VP-operator, not an MV-operator. Another criterion is that if such an auxiliary as intransitive *can* (cf. pp. 71–72) is added, then the operation of *in a factory* can include this auxiliary, for it seems that what is in a factory can very well be the possibility of John working, not only his work ("possibility" is here used as a nominalized form of *can*). Moreover, *in a factory* does not take part in the subcategorization of the verb in the way MV-operators do. Cf. Chomsky 1965: 102 ff.

   The deep structure of fig. 4 resembles the surface structure of the following pair of sentences:

(10) The men were transported to another prison. The transportation was by bus.

   The reason why complex T_{adv} has not applied to (10) is that the VP tense feature of the second sentence is [+tn], not [−tn]. Cf. 1 (a) on p. 79.

   Case (e), i.e. MV-operation, is exemplified by the generation of *cheaply* in the S_4 of fig. 6 and, more in detail, in the S_{4a} of fig. 8. Note that the auxiliary *can* has here nothing to do with the underlying adjective *cheap*. It is the flying that is cheap, not the possibility to fly.

   All so-called manner adverbs are, however, not generated in this way, for some of them must be classified as S-operators and thus belong to case (a). One example of this is *enthusiastically* in *John described the plan enthusiastically*, which can be paraphrased as "John described the plan and was enthusiastic in doing so." In accordance with this paraphrase it can be given a deep structure such as that shown in fig. 5. S_3 is here a description of the relationship between S_1 and S_2 and is later erased entirely because of *it*-deletion and because of deletion due to the identity of S_4 and S_2 and of S_5 and S_1. The feature [+adv] of the Pred of S_3 is here specified as [+concomitant], meaning that S_2, i.e. John's enthusiasm, accompanied S_1, i.e. his description of the plan.

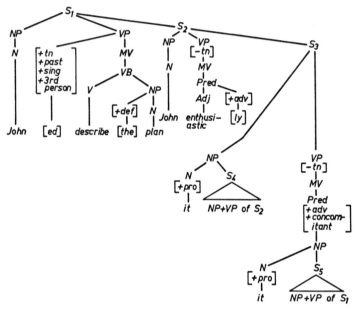

Fig. 5. The deep structure of *John described the plan enthusiastically.*

Rule (7) for the generation of dominated adverbial base sentences is recursive, i.e. it can be applied repeatedly, so that we may generate, for example, a sequence of three MV-dominated adverbial base sentences. This is illustrated in figs. 6 and 7, which show in a very simplified form the principle of MV-dominated recursiveness and its realization in surface structure. As can be clearly seen, the recursiveness is achieved by the possibility of using the optional Seq in the first line of rule (7).[7] Similar recursiveness can be achieved also in the case of S and VP domination.

---

[7] Cf. Bach 1967: 472: "It is possible that *Prep-phrase* should be considered as coming from a second sentence, to account for the fact that there is no reasonable limit on the number of such adverbials in one sentence."

86

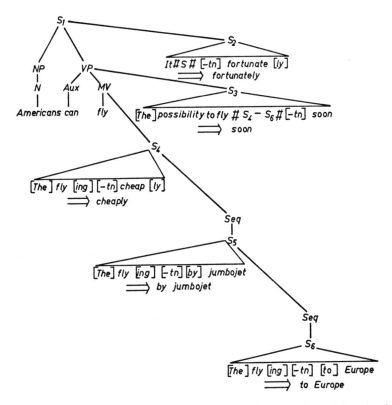

Fig. 6. Diagram illustrating in simplified form the generation of the adverbials in *Fortunately Americans can soon fly cheaply by jumbojet to Europe* with arrows indicating the results of adverbializations. The S that is embedded in S_2 is identical with S_1 (minus, of course, S_2 itself). The semantic content of S_3 can be expressed as "the possibility to fly cheaply by jumbojet to Europe soon".

In the sequence of MV-dominated adverbials the three components are not on the same structural level, for the modification of *fly* by *cheaply* is further specified by *by jumbojet*, whose modification, in its turn, is further specified by *to Europe*. By means of the rule schema mentioned in paper no. 5, footnote 5, a sequence of MV-dominated adverbial base sentences on the same structural level could be generated, but it would give the following peculiar surface structure

(11) *Americans can fly cheaply, by jumbojet, and to Europe.

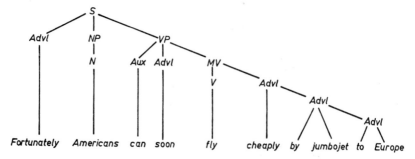

Fig. 7. The surface structure of the sentence generated in the way illustrated by fig. 6. Note that intra-nodal transportation (see (9)) of the adverbials derived from S_2 and S_3 has taken place.

It is, however, quite possible to use the rule schema in the generation of, for example, the following coordinated sequence

(12) Americans can fly cheaply, quickly, and safely.

Fig. 6 illustrates how a phrase-marker can contain not only a sequence of MV-dominated adverbial base sentences but also at the same time the base sentences of such adverbs as *fortunately* and *soon*, which are immediately dominated by S and VP, respectively. Thus the surface structure sentence *Fortunately Americans can soon fly cheaply by jumbojet to Europe* is generated. We can even go further and use the optional S in the expansion of S and MV in the first and third lines of rule (7) to generate adverbials that modify other adverbials. See fig. 8, which illustrates the generation of the string *probably extremely cheaply*, where *extremely* modifies *cheaply* and *probably* modifies *extremely cheaply*. If we include these operations, the ultimate result will be the surface structure sentence *Fortunately Americans can soon fly, probably extremely cheaply, by jumbojet to Europe.*

It should be noted that the adverbial base sentence that underlies *extremely* in fig. 8 is an MV-operator, which shows that from the point of view of deep structure there is no difference between the way in which *cheaply* modifies *fly* and the way in which *extremely* modifies the adjective that underlies *cheaply*. This is an indication of the affinity between verbs and adjectives in the deep structure, clearly observable in such pairs as *John lazes—John is lazy*; some modern linguists even treat them as the same category on this level and only distinguish them by means of different features. See Lakoff 1965: 0–15 and A-1 ff., Ross 1967 *a*: 58, and Jacobs and Rosenbaum 1968: 63.

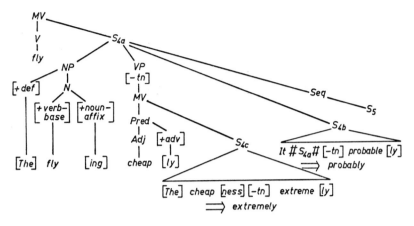

Fig. 8. Diagram illustrating how within the S₄ of fig. 6 the adverbs *probably* and *extremely* can be generated. After their generation they undergo transportation to the positions that they take up in surface structure, where the order is *probably extremely cheaply.*

Postscript

An approach to the generation of adverbials involving even more transformations than in this paper would be to assume that the adverbial base sentences described in section 2 have the same nodal adherence in deep structure and that they are moved transformationally to other nodes at different levels. Thus instead of basing the description on PS rules that contain optional S's, which are rewritten into adverbial base sentences, it is possible, by simply using the rule schema mentioned in footnote 5 of paper no. 5, to generate these adverbial base sentences as sentences attached by coordination to the highest S. At an early stage in the transformational cycle they are then moved to the positions assigned to them by the PS rules on which the description in the present paper is based.

For example, in the still deeper structure assumed in this way the following terminal strings would underlie those of figs. 2, 4, 5, and 8 in the present paper:

Fig. 2: John [s] know *and* it # John [s] know # [− tn] fortunate [ly]

Fig. 4: John [s] work *and* [the] work [ing] [− tn] [in] [a] factory.

Fig. 5: John [ed] describe [the] plan *and* John [− tn] enthusiastic [ly] *and* it # NP + VP of S₂ # [− tn] [+ concomitant] it # NP + VP of S₁ #

Fig. 8: Americans can fly *and* [the] fly [ing] [−tn] cheap [ly] *and* [the] cheap [ness] [−tn] extreme [ly] *and* it # [the] fly [ing] [−tn] cheap [ly] and [the] cheap [ness] [−tn] extreme [ly] # [−tn] probable [ly].

This approach is in line with the following slogan used in generative semantics: "Complements In, Modifiers Out", which means that whereas complements belong to a sentence from the deep structure onwards, modifiers are generated outside it. For further information see Jacobson (in preparation).

7. A Comparison Between Chomsky's Standard Theory and the Emergent Theory of Generative Semantics

Introduction

Since the publication of Noam Chomsky's *Aspects of the Theory of Syntax* in 1965 a new generative-transformational theory has appeared, which is often regarded as a reaction to some of the ideas laid down in that book. On the whole, however, it seems equally correct to describe it as an outgrowth and further development of Chomsky's theory. The main proponents of the new approach are Paul Postal, George Lakoff, John Robert Ross, and James D. McCawley. All of these have been disciples of Chomsky, and it therefore seems appropriate to speak about their grammar as neo-Chomskyan. They themselves usually call their new theory Generative Semantics. Sometimes, when they want to emphasize their very abstract approach to syntax, they also use the term Abstract Syntax. However, no independent status is assigned to syntax; it is more or less subsumed in the semantics. The opposite attitude, that syntax should be kept strictly apart from semantics, is called Autonomous Syntax; it was especially prevalent in the Structuralist School. In a forthcoming book entitled *Generative Semantics* George Lakoff attempts to outline what he calls a Basic Theory of Generative Semantics.

Chomsky, who took an active part in the revision which his original theory, as laid down in *Syntactic Structures* (1957), underwent round about 1965, has been less willing this time to adapt himself to new ideas. He has answered by only slightly modifying what he calls his Standard Theory in the form it appears in Chomsky 1965. The main modification is that the semantic component now interprets not only deep structure but also to some extent derived structure, especially surface structure (see Chomsky 1968: 35). As the semantic component is not regarded as generative but only in-terpretive, the Standard Theory and other theories that share this view are often referred to as Interpretivism. Another further development is the special treatment Chomsky gives to derived nominals by accommodating them directly in the base and rejecting the possibility of transformations changing the categorial status of the lexical items from which they are derived. This approach is called Lexicalism.

Adherents of Generative Semantics who think that the interpretivist and lexicalist approach is more superficial than their own refer to it derogatorily as Surfacism.

I will now examine some aspects of generative-transformational grammar where major differences can be found between Chomsky's modified Standard Theory and the neo-Chomskyan theory of Generative Semantics. The description of the latter draws heavily on lectures given by McCawley and Ross and on Lakoff's forthcoming book mentioned above.

1. The General Organization of the Grammar

(a) *Chomsky's Modified Standard Theory*

The type of transformational grammar assumed in Chomsky's modified Standard Theory is graphically depicted in fig. 1. According to Chomsky 1968: 5–7, a transformational grammar may be regarded as a hypothetical model of either competence or performance. In the former case no order is to be assigned to the components as the grammar simultaneously generates quadruples consisting of phonetic representation, surface structure, deep structure, and semantic representation, which are mapped onto each other without any special direction. A hypothetical performance model, on the other hand, describes the production of speech (or writing), and in this case order is essential. Fig. 1 is thus a model of the former type. It may be explained as follows.

The linguistic competence of a human being enables him or her to turn a message into a linguistic form (the speaker's or writer's role) and, vice versa, to turn a linguistic form into a message (the listener's or reader's role). In Chomsky's competence model the message is given an abstract linguistic form by the base of the syntactic component. This base generates deep structures by means of PS (=phrase-structure) rules, subcategorization rules, and a lexicon. The "words" of the lexicon are at this stage represented by phonological and syntactic feature matrices. For a matrix of the former type see fig. 2 and of the latter type fig. 7.

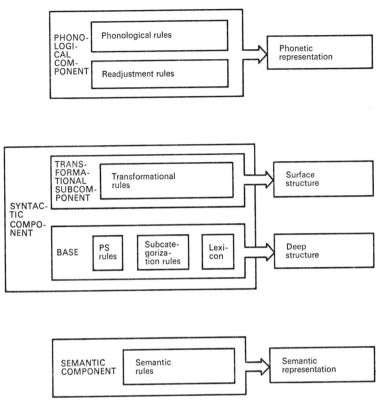

Fig. 1. Competence model of the transformational grammar assumed by Chomsky's Modified Standard Theory.

The deep structures are interpreted in the semantic component by means of so-called projection rules, which assign "readings" to all constituents. Such projection rules have been described, for example, by Katz and Postal 1964: 12 ff. Chomsky himself has, however, been blamed for not having sufficiently specified what the rules of the semantic component are to look like or how they are to operate (see, for instance, McCawley 1967: 14).

The deep structures are also the input of the transformational subcomponent, which by means of its T (=transformational) rules give rise to a series of intermediate structures with surface structures as their end product. These, in their turn, are the input of the phonological component. The T rules are cyclic, which means that they are applied "from the bottom up" beginning with the deepest embedded sentences and then pro-

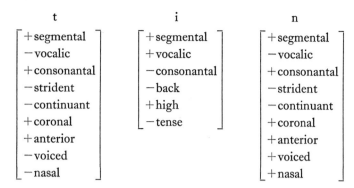

Fig. 2. Phonological distinctive feature matrix of the word *tin* in the lexicon. Cf. Chomsky–Halle 1968: 167–77.

ceeding sequentially to higher sentences (Chomsky 1965: 134–35 and 143). Some transformations are last-cyclic, i.e. they apply only to a whole phrase-marker (cf. Lakoff 1966: 34, Chomsky 1968: 38, and Jackendoff 1968: 13).

Intermediate and surface structures are also to some extent interpreted by the semantic component, for according to Chomsky 1968: 35 "such matters as focus and presupposition, topic and comment, reference, scope of logical elements and perhaps other phenomena are determined in part at least by structures ... other than deep structures, in particular by properties of surface structure." See also Jackendoff 1968: 10.

(b) *The Theory of Generative Semantics*

In Generative Semantics a grammar is regarded as a set of constraints on permissible derivations. The perhaps most striking difference between the grammar of this theory and that of Chomsky's theory is that it has no separate syntactic and semantic components. Instead it has a base component, which is both semantic and syntactic. For this reason the grammar only generates triples consisting of semantic representation, surface structure, and phonetic representation, and not quadruples as Chomsky's grammar does. Moreover, Chomsky's conception of a post-lexical deep structure is rejected, and the term deep structure is only accepted as another designation for semantic representation. McCawley says (1967:17–18) that ever since Chomsky introduced the notion of deep structure "virtually every 'deep structure' which has been postulated (excluding those which have been demonstrated simply to be wrong) has turned out not really to be a deep structure but to have underlying it a more abstract structure which could more appropriately be called the 'deep structure' of the sentence in question."

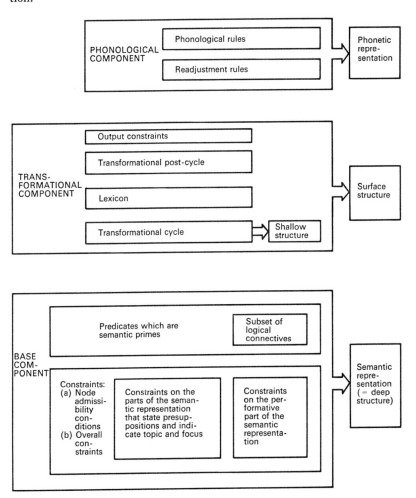

Fig. 3. Competence model of the transformational grammar assumed by the Theory of Generative Semantics.

Just as in the case of Chomsky's theory, a hypothetical model of the grammar of Generative Semantics can be either a nondirectional competence model or a directional performance model. Fig. 3, which depicts a model of the former type, can be explained as follows from the point of view of our human competence to give a message a linguistic form.

The base component assigns to this message a semantic representation in the form of a phrase-marker, whose nodal well-formedness is regulated by special constraints called node admissibility conditions. Other so-called overall constraints regulate, for example, the notion of commanding (Ross 1967 a: 259–60). The semantic representation includes a performative part, i.e. a part dominated by a sentence with a performative verb, which is usually deleted (see Ross 1968), and parts stating presuppositions or indicating topic and focus. The label of a terminal node may be a referential index, either in the form of a constant denoted by an alphabet-initial letter such as a, b, or c, or a variable denoted by an alphabet-final letter such as x, y, or z. All these letters can be subscripted by numbers, e.g. c_3, so that an infinite set of constants and variables is obtained. Constants refer to the special things that one is talking about, whereas variables range over the members of some set under discussion.[1] If, however, the terminal node is dominated by a predicate, its label is a semantic prime. This is the designation for an "atomic word", i.e. a word which is indivisible syntactically and semantically. The label of a predicate is usually V for "verb", but the prime that it dominates is not necessarily a verb. It can, for example, be a predicative noun or adjective, a quantifier such as *all*, or even a logical connective such as *and*.

The semantic representations, or deep structures, generated by the base component are the input of the transformational component. Just as in the case of Chomsky's theory, this component generates intermediate structures with surface structures as their end product. It has, however, two sets of ordered T rules, cyclic and post-cyclic.[2] All the former rules are applied in sequence first to the deepest embedded sentence, then all of them are applied in the same way to the next higher sentence, etc., and the intermediate structures that are the result of them are called shallow structures. In the case of the latter rules, all applications of one transformation precede all applications of the next transformation. For further information, see Mc-

---

[1] It should be noted that quantifiers only bind variables. Thus McCawley (1969 c: 6) uses only variables when distinguishing the two readings of *One of you is clearly lying*, namely
Clear (One_x (x is lying; x among 'you'))
to mean "It is clear that there is one of you who is lying" and
One_x (Clear (x is lying); x among 'you')
to mean "There is one of you such that it is clear that he is lying", although in the latter case we have a specific person that is being talked about, not any member of the set 'you'.
[2] McCawley (1970: 286) claims that one pre-cyclic transformation also exists, namely "the sentence pronominalization which gives rise to the *it* of such sentences as *Margaret is believed by many to be pregnant but she denies it.*"

Cawley 1970: 286–88. The transformations, or as they are also called, the local derivational constraints, of the transformational component can be based not only on an immediately preceding phrase-marker, but also on more deeply lying phrase-markers. There are also constraints on what is a possible surface structure, so-called output constraints, which, for example, exclude certain double negatives in standard English.[3] The transformational component contains the lexicon, and certain evidence has been adduced in favor of the assumption that lexical insertion takes place in the transformational cycle (Binnick et al. 1968: 23). The lexical items and the semantic primes on which they are based are represented by phonological feature matrices of the same type as that depicted in fig. 2.

The phonological component is on the whole the same as in Chomsky's Standard Theory. One difference is that the readjustment rules would, for example, operate on a predicate with a terminal node labeled *past* instead of the syntactic feature [− Pres], for Generative Semantics does not include features of this type (see below).

2. Certain Details of the Grammatical Description

(a) *PS Rules versus Node Admissibility Conditions*

The phrase-structure rules of Chomsky's theory are rewrite rules of the type of the now classic formula S→NP⁀VP. The structures generated by these rules can be rendered graphically in the form of phrase-markers or by means of labeled bracketing (fig. 4). Chomsky's own conception of what category labels are to be used in such formulas has differed from time to time. For

(a)   (b)

Fig. 4. Phrase-marker (*a*) and labeled bracketing (*b*) rendering the Chomskyan rewrite rule S→NP⁀VP.

---

[3] The output constraints are a type of level constraints, as they apply to the level of surface structure. For an interesting discussion about the role of output constraints, or, as Perlmutter calls them, surface structure constraints, see Perlmutter 1968: 233.

Besides level constraints (such as the output constraints and the various constraints of the base component) and the local derivational constraints of the transformational component a grammar also has global derivational constraints, which regulate, for example, the ordering of T rules.

example, in certain parts of Chomsky 1965, S is rewritten as NP^Aux^V (e.g. p. 85), in others as NP^Predicate-Phrase (e.g. p. 106). In Chomsky 1967: 27–28 a revision is suggested, which would give the same rewrite rule the form S→N̿ V̿.

The node admissibility conditions of Generative Semantics do not like rewrite rules generate strings from which trees can be derived; instead they generate trees directly. These node admissibility conditions have been inspired by the predicate calculus of symbolic logic, which divides a proposition into a predicate and one or more arguments.[4] A proposition node is labeled S (=sentence), a predicate node V (=verb), and an argument node NP (=noun phrase). The order in predicate calculus is retained so that we obtain phrase-markers of the type shown in fig. 5. This order, which appears in the surface structure of VSO languages, is considered more basic than the SVO order of English surface structure (McCawley 1970).

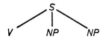

Fig. 5. A phrase-marker in Generative Semantics with a two-place predicate, i.e. a predicate with two arguments, as in the sentence *John knows the answer.*

The node admissibility condition that generates the phrase-marker of fig. 5 looks as follows:

$$\langle S; V\ NP^n\rangle\ n \geqslant 1$$

This may be read, "A tree configuration with a node labeled S immediately and exclusively dominating a node labeled V and at least one node labeled NP is well-formed." In the set of node admissibility conditions there is also one of the form

$$\langle NP; S\rangle$$

by means of which we can obtain a phrase-marker configuration where an NP immediately dominates an S, as in fig. 6. This figure, in which I have

---

[4] The close links between Generative Semantics and natural logic are demonstrated in G. Lakoff 1970. McCawley (personal communication) claims that in his work on Generative Semantics he has not started with a fixed version of logical structure and fitted grammar to it but chosen among alternative versions of logic (e.g. not everybody's logical notation involves predicates coming first) and among alternative versions of syntax and come up with a single proposal that appears to work for both the logician's and the syntactician's purposes.

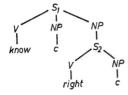

Fig. 6. A subtree in Generative Semantics showing part of the deep structure of *John* (=c) *knows that he is right.* The V of S_2 is an example of a one-place predicate.

simply assumed that *know* and *right* are semantic primes, shows only a sub-tree of the performative part of the deep structure; dominating it are other sentences, one of which contains a performative V, e.g. *tell,* with the speaker as subject-NP, and another a V indicating tense. Moreover, in the presuppositional part of the deep structure there is a subtree of the following content, "I assume that there is a c, such that c is called John."

As has already been pointed out, the number of category symbols in Chomsky's grammar is quite large. Besides S and NP, there are, for example, such symbols as N (=noun), Det (=determiner), VP (=verb phrase), V (=verb), Aux (=auxiliary), M (=modal), Adj (=adjective), and Manner (=manner adverb). In Generative Semantics the number of category symbols is limited to three: S, V, and NP. This reduction has been achieved by subsuming under V and NP a number of linguistic elements which are regarded as separate categories by Chomsky (as regards what is subsumed under V see 1*b*, 3rd par., above). Such subsumption is made possible by increasing the number of sentences composing a deep structure so that earlier categories such as tense auxiliaries can be placed as independent V's in sentences of their own. For a further discussion of the category reduction, see McCawley 1969*a*.

(b) *Syntactic Features and Morphemes versus Tree Configurations*

In Chomsky's theory subcategorization rules are of two types: strict subcategorization rules and selectional rules. Together with the PS rules, which perform the main categorization, these two sets of rules give rise to the system of syntactic features which constitute a complex symbol (Chomsky 1965: 84). Like the phonological features in fig. 2. the syntactic features are preceded by plus or minus. See fig. 7.

Besides category symbols and syntactic features Chomsky-type phrase-markers often contain various syntactic morphemes such as Q for question and I for imperative, which have the purpose of triggering transformations (see, for example, Katz and Postal 1964: 76 and 79).

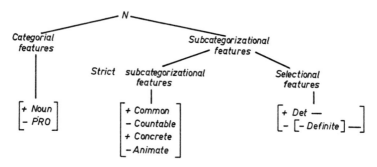

Fig. 7. Complex symbol (= syntactic feature representation) of the mass-word *tin* in a Chomskyan phrase-marker. The categorial features correspond to categories generated by PS rules, whereas the subcategorizational features are generated directly by subcategorization rules. [− PRO] means that the noun in question is not a PRO form such as *one, body,* or *thing.* The selectional features indicate that the word can take determiners in general, e.g. *the, some,* but not the indefinite article. The dash denotes the place of the noun.

Generative Semantics has neither syntactic features nor syntactic morphemes of this kind.[5] The reason is that they are considered too arbitrary, and accordingly this type of Chomskyan grammar is often referred to as Arbitrary Syntax.

Instead of strict subcategorizational features Generative Semantics uses predicates which are part of ordinary sentential tree configurations of the type shown in figures 5 and 6. For example, the strict subcategorizational features in fig. 7 are replaced by a subtree such as that depicted in fig. 8. The content of this subtree may be read, "b_1 (i.e. the referential index used in the phrase-marker until lexical insertion of the mass-word *tin* takes place on the basis of this subtree and other subtrees specifying the semantic content of the word, e.g. that it is a metal) is not individual, it is concrete, and it is inanimate."[6] Semantic features are treated in the same way, and thus the

---

[5] The only features that exist in Generative Semantics are rule exception features (McCawley, personal communication).

[6] As regards the feature [+common] McCawley (personal communication) says that " 'commonness' will be predictable from something else that appears in semantic structure, namely whether the semantic structure simply consists of a sentence 'x is called X' or not." The nonpresence of a branch meaning "b_1 is called Tin" in the phrase-marker of which fig. 8 depicts a subtree, is thus sufficient indication that b_1 is common. About the feature [−countable] he says that "it isn't going to correspond to an embedded sentence 'b_1 cannot be counted', since everyone knows that you can count grains of rice as easily as you can count beans. The difference is going

slender distinction made by Chomsky between syntactic subcategorizational features and semantic features is leveled out. See (c), 1st par., below.

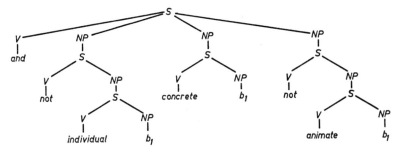

Fig. 8. Subtree of a phrase-marker in Generative Semantics corresponding to the Chomskyan strict subcategorizational feature column of fig. 7. Some of the predicates of this subtree are further divisible, i.e. they are not true semantic primes.

Selectional syntactic features denoting, for example, that the mass-word *tin* can take determiners such as *the* or *some* or that the verb *pretend* must have a subject that is animate are replaced in Generative Semantics by general presuppositions about the normal state of things of the world we live in. It would, for example, be considered anomalous for anyone to count a nonindividual mass or for a stone to pretend. Such sentences are therefore automatically rejected (cf. Binnick et al. 1968: 16–19). One consequence of this approach is that Generative Semantics treats pragmatics not as extralinguistic but as an integral part of its linguistic system. It should be pointed out, however, that a sentence like "The stone pretends that it is a cow" is anomalous only from the point of view of the beliefs we have about our normal world, for we can very well create a fairy-tale or dream world in which stones can pretend.

Syntactic morphemes like Q and I are also replaced by tree configurations like those shown in figures 5 and 6 in the form of performative sentences which dominate the part of the deep structure that underlies what is actually uttered. Thus "Is John ill" and "Go!" are derived from deep structures the

---

to be whether the word refers to the individuation of the substance or not, not whether such an individuation exists in nature or is possible." It is the concept of individuation in this case that I have tried to render by including in fig. 8 a branch meaning "b_1 is not individual".

contents of which can be read, "I request of you that you tell me whether John is ill" and "I request of you that you go." For a simplified phrase-marker of the deep structure of the latter sentence, see fig. 9. By changing the performative verb *request* into, for example, *entreat* or *demand* various shades of meaning can be rendered.

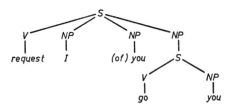

Fig. 9. Simplified deep structure of *Go!* in Generative Semantics.

(c) *Lexical Insertion*

In Chomsky's theory the lexicon consists of an unordered set of lexical entries and certain redundancy rules. Each lexical entry consists of a phonological distinctive feature matrix of the type shown in fig. 2 and a complex symbol, which is a set of syntactic and semantic features. The syntactic features match those which are developed by PS and subcategorization rules in the form of a complex symbol in a phrase-marker (fig. 7). The semantic features have been little discussed by Chomsky; roughly they are of the same type as the strict subcategorizational features. The line between these and semantic features must be difficult to draw, and Chomsky admits that he simply calls a feature semantic if "it is not mentioned in any syntactic rule" (Chomsky 1965: 142). The redundancy rules of the lexicon state general properties of all lexical entries and thus eliminate from the individual entries what can be predicted, so that concentration can be made on what is idiosyncratic. Lexical insertion is regarded as a substitution transformation by which the phonological feature matrices of lexical entries replace the complex symbols of phrase-markers.

Generative Semantics, too, regards lexical insertion as a transformational process. However, it has no system of syntactic and semantic features, so what is replaced by a lexical item is instead a constituent or subtree of a phrase-marker (cf. McCawley 1968b: 72). Thus the lexical item *boy* in the form of a phonological distinctive feature matrix such as that in fig. 2 is substituted for the subtree in fig. 10. Part of this subtree is the result of a conjunction reduction transformation performed on a deep structure that can be assumed to be of the form depicted in fig. 11. Here we have assumed for the sake of the discussion that the predicates of the conjoined sentences are semantic primes.

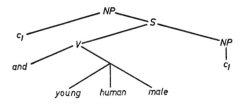

Fig. 10. Subtree of an intermediate phrase-marker in Generative Semantics for which the lexical item *boy* can be inserted.

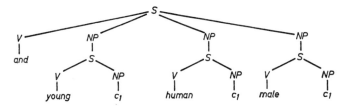

Fig. 11. Deep structure subtree in Generative Semantics, showing the assumed semantic primes on which the lexical item *boy* is based.

A different type of structure underlies such a lexical item as the transitive verb *break* in its past tense form *broke*. This structure can be assumed to include in one of its intermediate phrase-markers a subtree with the meaning "c_1 caused d_1 to break." The intransitive verb *break* that appears here in its turn seems to be decomposable into the smaller units "become not whole." In the semantic representation the structure underlying the transitive verb *break* in its past tense form can therefore be assumed to have the shape shown in fig. 12. This structure cannot be directly transformed into the form *broke* as it also includes the two indices c_1 and d_1. Therefore a cyclic predicate-raising transformation has to be applied, by which *whole* is raised into S_4, then *not whole* into S_3, then *become not whole* into S_2, and finally *cause become not whole* into S_1. After raising also the NP dominating c_1 into S_1 and "pruning" the tree of the now unnecessary nodes S_2, S_3, S_4, and S_5 together with their NP's, we obtain the intermediate structure of fig. 13. Here V_2 dominates only semantic material entering into the transitive verb *break* and is thus a constituent that can be replaced by the phonological distinctive feature matrix for this verb. It is possible that the lexical insertion proceeds stepwise, so that the transitive verb is inserted only after previous insertion of the intransitive verb for the V_3 constituent.

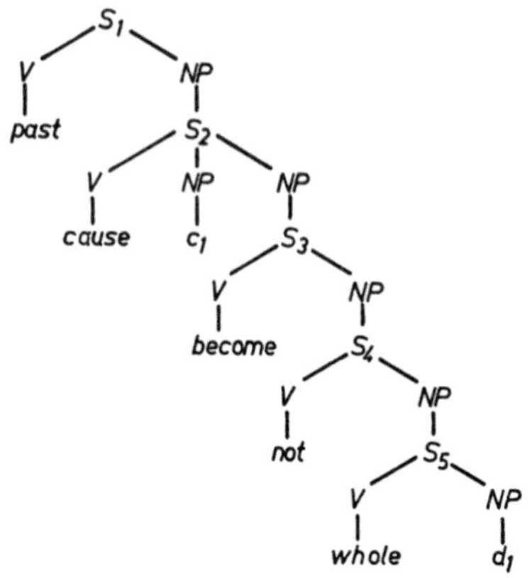

Fig. *12*. Deep structure subtree in Generative Semantics assumed to underlie the transitive verb *break* in its past tense form (cf. McCawley 1968*b*: 73–74 and Binnick et al. 1968: 21).

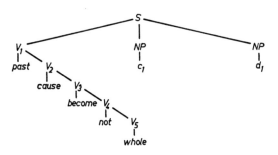

Fig. *13*. The intermediate structure of the subtree in fig. 12 just before lexical insertion of the transitive verb *break* for V_2–V_5.

Let us now assume that the two lexical insertions described above have been performed on the intermediate structure of the sentence "The boy broke the window." Then, after inserting *window* for a constituent including the semantic material of d_1, we obtain a shallow structure of the form shown in fig. 14.

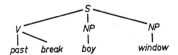

Fig. 14. The shallow structure of the sentence *The boy broke the window* in Generative Semantics.

What happens in the further derivational history of our sentence is, firstly, that definite articles are inserted before *boy* and *window*. I will venture a suggestion that this insertion is at least partially due to the fact that the referential indices for both these nouns are constants, thus denoting the special things that one is talking about (cf. 1 (*b*), 3rd par., above).[7] Secondly, the shallow structure undergoes word-order change in the post-cycle, so that the surface structure of fig. 15 is obtained.

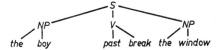

Fig. 15. The surface structure of the sentence *The boy broke the window.*

The constituent *past break* of this surface structure is changed into *broke* by the readjustment rules of the phonological component, and phonological rules give the word *boy* strong stress if the semantic representation indicates that c_1 is in focus. A stronger form of the same focus indication would have given rise to the cleft sentence "It was the boy who broke the window (not, for example, the girl)."

Conclusion

Admittedly the theory of Generative Semantics is still only in the initial stages of its development and many of its tenets have been subjected to criticism, but the description of it that has so far been given seems to indicate that it has at least certain advantages over Chomsky's theory.

One is the uniform nature both of graphical representations and of rules. Thus semantic as well syntactic representations are of the form of labeled

---

[7] According to McCawley (personal communication) no generative semanticist has so far made any concrete proposal as to how articles are derived or how sentences with definite and indefinite articles differ in semantic structure.

trees, and there is a single system of rules, namely transformations, which relate deep structure to surface structure. Chomsky's Standard Theory, on the other hand, has one set of rules, namely transformations, linking deep structure and surface structure and another set, namely projection rules, linking deep structure and semantic representation.[8] The building blocks used in constructing the graphical representations in Generative Semantics are simple in that only three category labels are involved, whereas Chomsky's theory has a large variety of such labels.

Another advantage is that it feels intuitively correct to base a grammar on the content of a message rather than on a syntactic rewrite rule such as S→NP^VP. It is true that as far as a competence model is concerned the order in which the components are discussed in the generation of sentences is not meant to indicate directionality, but I think one can agree with Lyons 1970: 796 that it reflects different attitudes to deep structure in that Generative Semantics can be understood as implying that this structure is to a considerable extent determined by meaning whereas this is not so in the case of Chomsky's interpretivist theory.

According to Generative Semantics, it is not possible to draw sharp lines of demarcation between syntax and semantics, and genuine adherents of this theory would deny that there are any judgments of grammaticality that do not involve semantic judgments (cf. McCawley 1967: 55). For example, whereas Chomsky would be likely to say that *Golf plays John* is ungrammatical, Binnick (1969: 4) maintains that any judgment must depend on what this statement is supposed to mean, for Golf might be the name of a person and John the name of a new game, or the idea might be that John has become such a golf-addict that the game plays him rather than the other way round. If, on the other hand, the idea is "John plays golf", then the statement must be described as ill-formed as it does not succeed in conveying the message intended, and this description, too, is based on a judgment involving meaning.

It is true to say that Generative Semantics has enhanced the role of semantics in grammar by thus placing it on the same level as syntax, but it is equally true to say that Generative Semantics has shown that syntax is strongly involved also in cases which were earlier thought to be of a primarily seman-

---

[8] In a lecture at Stockholm University just before the publication of the present volume it was claimed by Jerrold Katz that the projection rules are actually transformational rules, the difference being merely notational, and that in a similar way other points of controversy between the two theories could also be simply reduced to notational differences. Cf. Katz 1970.

tic nature. For example, it has been established in the present paper that such monomorphemic lexical items as *boy* and *break* are not only semantically different, but differ in their underlying syntactic structure to a much greater extent than is indicated by the simple syntactic division into noun and transitive verb.

It is likely that these deeper insights into the syntactic and semantic relationships of utterances will add to our knowledge of how translation from one language to another should be carried out. The deep structures of Generative Semantics are intended to be of a universal nature, as they are based on human thought, but there will naturally be differences between languages as people with different linguistic backgrounds do not think in exactly the same way. Thus Lappish has several words for mountain, and it depends on the shape of the mountain which word is used in each case. The tree configuration for the word *mountain* in a particular sentence will therefore as a rule contain more semantic material in Lappish than in the corresponding English sentence. In translation we can choose to ignore this difference, i.e. we can simply leave certain parts of the Lappish tree configuration untranslated, but we can also choose to place this semantic material elsewhere in the sentence in the form of, for example, descriptive adjectives.

Finally it ought to be pointed out that the purpose of Generative Semantics is not restricted to Chomsky's rather mechanical goal of generating all and only the grammatical sentences of a language. Instead Generative Semantics gives generation free rein within the limits of human thought, keeping in mind that even strings which look deviant under normal circumstances can in certain contexts convey meanings which are understood by at least some people.

8. Five Categories of Tense

Introduction

Many grammatical concepts can be looked at from a logical as well as from a formal point of view. Thus in a passive sentence we have a formal subject, which agrees with the finite verb, but also a logical subject, which when expressed appears in the so-called agent. On similar lines we may divide tense into logical tense and formal tense. This binary division bears a certain resemblance to the division into deep and surface tense that is propounded by Huddleston (1969). In this paper I will discuss the four categories mentioned and add to them a fifth, namely intermediate tense. I would like to distinguish the five categories briefly as follows.

Logical tense denotes logical time relations, for example, the relation between a verbal process (=action, event, or state) and a certain temporal expression (and/or situation of utterance), or the relation between two or more verbal processes.

Formal tense is characterized by various bound or free morphemes, such as *-ed* and *have*, or by special stem forms, such as *are* and *came*. A logical tense may be left formally unexpressed, as in *John's arrival*. On the other hand, a formal tense may express more than just temporal relations, as in

(1) I wish it was true.,

where the formal past tense expresses not only logical present time but also unreality.

Deep tense is logical tense in the abstract formalized version that is used in the deep structure representation of sentences in transformational grammar.

Intermediate tense is a single occurrence, or a combination, of the tense predicates *past*, *present*, and *future*, which are generated in low intermediate structure by a special reduplication transformation on the basis of deep tense.

A term covering both deep tense and various stages of intermediate tense is underlying tense. In this paper I do not regard this as a designation for a special category.

Surface tense is generated by various transformations of intermediate tense, and is actually the same thing as formal tense looked upon from the point of view of generation.

The relationship between the five types of tense discussed above is graphically depicted in fig. 1.

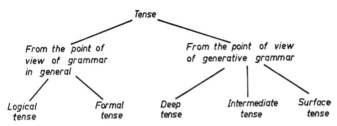

Fig. 1. The relationship between the five types of tense discussed in this paper.

I will now discuss what determines logical and formal tense and how deep, intermediate, and surface tense are generated.

1. Factors Determining Logical Tense

Logical tense is determined by such factors as the following.

1.1. *Deictic elements which indicate the particular temporal situation of the linguistic performance (= the act of speaking or writing).*

Examples of such elements are adverbials like *at present, right now,* and *today.* A sentence can also be related to the time of the linguistic performance by means of the pronoun I + a performative verb, such as *declare, tell,* or *request,* as in "I declare you man and wife".

1.2. *Deictic elements which refer to temporal situations preceding or following the linguistic performance.*

Such elements are, for example, the adverbs *yesterday* and *tomorrow,* which denote past and future, respectively, in relation to the time of speaking or writing. Time adverbials denoting fixed dates change their indication. Thus *in 1969* is future in relation to a linguistic performance taking place in 1968 but past in relation to one taking place in 1970.

1.3. *Various time-relational clauses and expressions denoting systematic grammatical contrasts.*[1]

These are introduced by, for example, *before, prior to* (one verbal process precedes another); *while, simultaneous with* (simultaneous verbal processes); *after, following, subsequent to* (one verbal process follows another). Systematic temporal relations are also expressed by an adverb series such as *first—then —finally* or the deleted or retained *and* that introduces consecutive events,[2] as in

(2) He walked up to the prisoner, looked at him contemptuously, raised his gun, and shot him.

Here we can also include catenatives (i.e. finite verbs followed by non-finite verbs), which place the time of the process expressed by the verbs following them in a particular relation to their own time. For example, the processes associated with the verbs following the catenatives *remember, keep,* and *intend* are placed in times which are, respectively, prior to, simultaneous with, and subsequent to, the times associated with these catenatives, as in

(3) (i) I remember seeing him.
  (ii) He keeps running.
  (iii) He intends coming.

The logical tense described in 1.1 above is unitary, that in 1.2 binary, and that in 1.3 ternary, as indicated by fig. 2.

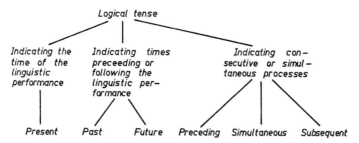

Fig. 2. The subcategorization of logical tense.

---

[1] Not all linguists would agree that the clauses and expressions discussed in this subsection denote tense, but in my opinion they conform to the following definition of tense given by Lyons 1968: 304: "The category of *tense* has to do with time-relations in so far as these are expressed by systematic grammatical contrasts."
[2] For a discussion of this type of *and*, see Staal 1968 and McCawley 1969b: 19–20.

2. Factors Determining Formal Tense

Formal tense is determined by such factors as the following.

2.1. *Logical tense.*

The logical tense discussed in 1.1 and 1.2 is rendered by formal tense when the verb denoting the verbal process is finite, as in (4) (i), or when the tense form can be attached to some finite auxiliary, as in (4) (ii).

(4)   (i) John loves me.
      (ii) I am loved by John.

In both these examples it is the process of loving that is logically in the present, and the auxiliary *am* in (ii), whose main function is to denote the passive, is a purely formal tense-marker.

Some auxiliaries, however, which have tense-marking as their main function, take an integral part in expressing logical tense when they are combined with non-finite verbs to make up special composite formal tenses, e.g. the present perfect in

(5) I have seen him.

Such composite formal tenses correspond to combinations of two or more logical tenses. For example, the present perfect is a combination of a logical present tense and a logical past tense, and the future past perfect combines one logical future tense and two logical past tenses, where one precedes the other.

Non-finite verbs can also denote certain formal tense differences on their own, for example by contrasting their simple and compound forms, as in

(6)   (i) Doing the job he was happy.
      (ii) Having done the job he was happy.

These differences are, however, often logically inadequate, as when in a sentence like

(7) He may have done it yesterday.,

a non-finite present perfect tense is combined with an adverb such as *yesterday*, which from a logical point of view places the action entirely in the past.

Formally tenseless are verb-based nouns, such as *arrival* or *description*. Thus all the following occurrences of *John's arrival* are ambiguous as to whether the arrival is in the past, the present, or the future in relation to the linguistic performance. (This can be tested by introducing such post-nominal modifiers of *John's arrival* as *yesterday, now at 1 o'clock,* and *tomorrow*.)

(8) (i) John's arrival has caused a lot of trouble.
(ii) John's arrival is causing a lot of trouble.
(iii) John's arrival will cause a lot of trouble.

Similarly, there is as a rule no special formal tense that marks a verbal process as logically simultaneous or consecutive in relation to another (see 1.3 above). Thus no formal marker indicates that the time associated with the verb *coming* in the following examples is subsequent to that associated with the catenative *intend*:

(9) (i) He intends coming.
(ii) He intended coming.

Moreover, the consecutiveness of the habitual actions expressed by the two verbs in

(10) First Mary leaves, then John arrives.

is signalled only by the adverbs *first – then* and no formal tense distinction is made. If, however, we use the conjunctions *before* and *after* instead of the adverbs *first–then*, the interesting situation arises that in the case of *before* the notion of consecutiveness can be reinforced by the use of the present perfect in either the principal clause or the subordinate clause, whereas in the case of *after* the present perfect is restricted to the subordinate clause:

(11)   (i) Before John arrives, Mary leaves.
(ii) Before John arrives, Mary has left.
(iii) Before John has arrived, Mary leaves.

(12)   (i) Mary leaves before John arrives.
(ii) Mary has left before John arrives.
(iii) Mary leaves before John has arrived.

(13)   (i) After Mary leaves, John arrives.
(ii) After Mary has left, John arrives.
(iii) *After Mary leaves, John has arrived.

(14)   (i) John arrives after Mary leaves.
(ii) John arrives after Mary has left.
(iii) *John has arrived after Mary leaves.

In the examples numbered (i) the notion of consecutive action is rendered only by the use of *before* and *after*, respectively, whereas in those numbered

(ii) the use of the different formal tenses, the present perfect and the present, where the former denotes preceding action in relation to the latter, reinforces this notion. In the examples numbered (iii), however, the use of the two tenses is contradictory to the use of *before* and *after*. Then *before* has the power to overrule the consecutive relationship between the two tenses, whereas *after* has no such effect. A plausible reason for this difference may be that the presence of *before* and the present perfect in the same clause in (11) (iii) and (12) (iii) gives an impression of a reinforced notion of precedence, although logically the opposite holds true.

2.2. *The axis of orientation.*

Formal tense orders a verbal process with respect to a point of reference, which may be called the axis of orientation (cf. Huddleston 1969: 790). This axis is usually deictic (see 1.1 and 1.2), and it is on the basis of a deictic axis that the subcategorization of formal tense is made. See figures 3 and 4, where the terms pre-deictic, zero-deictic, and post-deictic mean in relation to a time which, respectively, precedes, covers, and follows the linguistic performance.

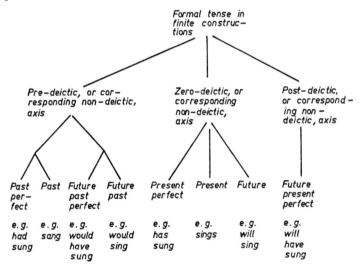

Fig. 3. The subcategorization of formal tense in English finite constructions. A simple future with a post-deictic axis is missing; instead the zero-deictic future acts as a "present future", which predicts future events with the axis in the present. See the discussion about (32), and cf. Huddleston 1969: 789 and Ruin 1970: 10 (= Bull 1960: 31).

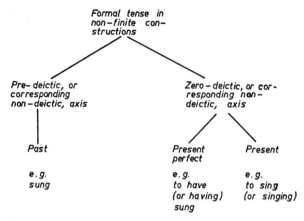

Fig. 4. The subcategorization of formal tense in English non-finite constructions.

When the axis is non-deictic, it is established not on the basis of the time of the linguistic performance but by reference either to the infinite time of a general truth or belief, e.g. "Man proposes, God disposes", or to the time of the verbal process of some contextual clause. As figures 3 and 4 show, the same subcategorization as in the case of a deictic axis applies in corresponding cases of a non-deictic axis.

If the axis is based on the tense of some other, non-performative clause, the axis is said to be dependent.[3] For example, the axis of a subordinate clause can be dependent on the tense of the matrix clause, i.e. the next higher clause, and the tense of a main clause can be dependent on the tense of a preceding main or subordinate clause.[4] Cf. Huddleston (1969: 796), who, however relates the dependent/independent dichotomy only to the matrix clause, a definition which I regard as too narrow.

The following example contains a subordinate clause with a dependent axis of orientation:

(15) He said that he would come tomorrow.

---

[3] Performative clauses are excepted, as these are instead involved in the deictic/non-deictic dichotomy. Thus the tense of the *that*-clause in "I declare that you are wrong" has a deictic relationship to the performative main clause but is otherwise independent of it.
[4] An example of the latter type is the following example given by Mary Gallagher (1970: 222):

The man who answered the telephone was my brother.

Here the axis of *was* is dependent on the tense of *answered*.

Here the formal tense of *would come* is the future past, which is oriented to the past tense form *said* in the matrix clause on which the *that*-clause depends. The logical tense of the *that*-clause, on the other hand, is the future, as is evident from the presence of the post-deictic adverb *tomorrow*. In the example

(16) He said that he will come tomorrow.,

logical and formal tense coincide for here the axis of the *that*-clause is independent of its matrix clause as regards tense.

The relationship between the different types of axis of orientation discussed is illustrated in fig. 5.

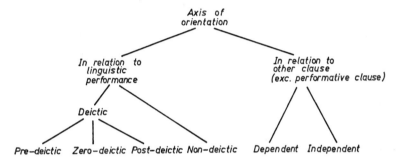

Fig. 5. Different types of axis of orientation.

A non-deictic axis can be independent, as in

(17) The sun rises in the east.

The tense of this sentence is not based on the time of the linguistic performance, as it is used in a statement about a general truth, and it does not depend on the tense of any contextual clause.

2.3. *Non-temporal grammatical phenomena, such as reality versus unreality or matter-of-factness versus politeness.*

For the purpose of denoting unreality a formal tense which differs from the corresponding logical tense is often used. Thus in the sentence

(18) I wish he was here now.,

the use of the illogical past tense form serves to convey the notion of un-reality. Special subjunctive forms can be used for the same purpose. Thus (18) can be replaced by

(19) I wish he were here now.

Occasionally there is ambiguity between a formal past denoting reality and one denoting unreality. This is, for example, the case in

(20) I'm sure that he could not do it.,

where the formal past tense form *could* can be interpreted as either "was able to" (reality) or "would be able to" (unreality). In the former case *could* is also logically a past tense, whereas in the latter it is a logical present tense.

In both the following examples the logical tense is the present. However, in the second a formal past tense form is used to make the question more polite than in the first, where the tone is more matter-of-fact.

(21) (i) Can I use your telephone?
      (ii) Could I use your telephone?

3. The Generation of Underlying Tense

As mentioned in the introduction to this paper the term "underlying tense" covers both deep tense and various stages of intermediate tense.

The generation of deep tense can be described in the transformational theory of generative semantics by means of semantic representations (= deep structures) which in tree-form express logical tense.[5] At the top of such a representation is placed a performative sentence, whose time is that of the act of speech or writing.[6] Lower down we find sentences, or other con-stituents, which underlie such temporal elements as express logical tense either on the basis of their systematic contrast to other temporal elements or on the basis of their relationship to the time of the linguistic performance.

According to McCawley 1969b: 2 ff. the deictic temporal relations ex-pressed by deep tense (cf. 1.1 and 1.2) are given duplex expression in the underlying structure by the addition of the tense predicates *past*, *present*, and

---

[5] For an account of the transformational theory of generative semantics and the differences between that theory and Chomsky's standard theory see paper no. 7.
[6] For illustration of performative sentences in semantic representations see fig. 6 of the present paper and fig. 9 of paper no. 7. See also Ross 1968.

future at an early stage of the transformational cycle. This addition is performed by a reduplication transformation. Mary Gallagher (1970: 224) has made a further suggestion which may be interpreted as signifying that in certain cases of logical tenselessness (as in (17), which neither refers to the time of the linguistic performance nor contains any temporal elements) the tense predicate *present* is introduced by a special rule.

McCawley maintains (1969*b*: 18 ff.) that the tense predicates introduced by reduplication are pronominal in nature in that they refer to contextual temporal expressions in a way that resembles the way in which personal pronouns refer to contextual nouns.

If the temporal expression is a time adverbial in the same clause, a tense predicate is actually redundant; this is the case, for example, in the underlying structure of the sentence

(22) I swam yesterday.

From a logical point of view this sentence would have been just as clear if it had been expressed as follows

(23) *I swim yesterday.,

in the same way as no formal tense distinguishes the future from the present in the two sentences

(24) (i) I am working today.
    (ii) I am working tomorrow.

This tense redundancy has a pronominal counterpart in such a sentence as

(25) Mr. Nixon, he is great.,

where *he* is redundant.

On the other hand, in a context such as

(26) "What did John do yesterday?"
    "He worked.",

where the answer "He worked" contains two instances of reference to antecedents, viz. *he*, which refers to *John*, and *-ed*, which refers to *yesterday*, the pronominalization of the noun and the addition of the tense predicate underlying *-ed* cannot be described as redundant, for they make it possible for us to avoid repeating the words *John* and *yesterday*. It is interesting to note in this connection that in a laconic answer to the question in (26) both *he* and *-ed* are omitted, not just one of them, i.e. the answer is "Work" not "He work" or "Worked".

A performative sentence, usually deleted in surface structure, fulfils the same function in triggering the transformation introducing a tense predicate as a time adverbial denoting the present time. Thus the present tense, formally denoted by *is* in

(27) John is swimming.,

is really redundant from a logical point of view, for the situation of utterance should be sufficient to make it clear that John's swimming is simultaneous with the speech act. It is only when reference is to some time that wholly or partially excludes the time of the linguistic performance that tense forms become necessary in the case of deleted or merely presupposed temporal expressions, as in

(28) (i) John was swimming.
     (ii) John has been swimming.

The temporal expressions underlying the tenses of these sentences must be assumed to have occurred earlier in the discourse or are simply presupposed by the speaker, for example, in the case of (28) (i) *yesterday* (logical past time) and in the case of (28) (ii) *from noon up to now* (where *from noon up to* denotes logical past time and *now* logical present time). See fig. 10, where the latter expression is presupposed.

The intermediate tense of a sentence such as (22) has only one tense predicate. A simplified deep structure and a simplified intermediate structure of this sentence after the addition of the tense predicate are shown in figures 6 and 7. The simplifications especially referred to in these phrase-markers and those that follow are the inclusion of all kinds of lexical items and other deviations from the strict cyclic order (p. 96). Actually only semantic primes can occur in deep structures and lower intermediate structures.

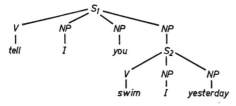

Fig. 6. Simplified deep structure of *I swam yesterday*. S_1 is a performative sentence, which later undergoes deletion so that only S_2 remains.

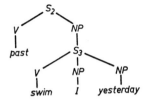

Fig. 7. Simplified intermediate structure of the S_2-dominated subtree of fig. 6 after a time adverbial reduplication transformation has inserted the tense predicate *past*.

Usually intermediate tense consists not of one but of two or more tense predicates. Thus two tense predicates underlie (27), whose deep structure and intermediate structure after tense predicate insertion are shown in simplified form in figs. 8 and 9. *Progressive* is here assumed to be a deep structure predicate, for which later the lexical item *be* is inserted. In all probability, however, it is further decomposable before its semantic primes are reached.[7]

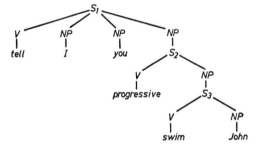

Fig. 8. Simplified deep structure of *John is swimming*.

Similarly three tense predicates underlie such a sentence as (28) (ii). See figs. 10 and 11. In the generation of these tense predicates the universal quantifier *all* occurring in the semantic representation plays an important role (cf. McCawley 1969 b: 10 ff.). This quantifier binding a variable denoting time gives the temporal range of the proposition, and in (28) (ii) this range includes the present. The time associated with the verbal process itself is, however, in the past in relation to the linguistic performance, and so is also

[7] I have suggested to Jan Nyvelius, Engl. Dept., Stockholm University, to investigate this matter as part of a research project on English aspect.

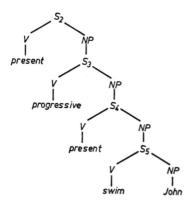

Fig. 9. Simplified intermediate structure of the S_2-dominated subtree of fig. 8 after addition of two instances of the tense predicate *present*.

the time associated with the progressive quality of this process.[8] The re-duplication transformation inserting tense predicates adds the predicate *present* to the range-indicating quantifier, which is then deleted, and the predicate *past* is added both to the predicate *progressive* and to the predicate *swim* with subsequent deletion of the time variable in both cases.

In the example just discussed the process of swimming is assumed to last up to the moment of the linguistic performance. However, the time associated with the verbal process and its progressiveness may very well be thought of as continuing also at that moment; this becomes especially evident if we add a *since*-expression:

(29) John has been swimming since noon.

Here the subtree corresponding to S_3–S_6 in fig. 11 can be rendered as a co-ordinate structure, as in fig. 12, where $S_{4.1}$ denotes the past activity and $S_{4.2}$ the present activity, their meanings being paraphrasable as "John began to swim at noon and is still swimming."

---

[8] Note that in the case of a present perfect expressing a repeated verbal process there can very well be a temporal gap between the last event and the moment of the linguistic performance, as in

I have been in England three times and plan to go there again next summer.

However, the temporal range of the proposition, i.e. the period within which the visits are regarded as having occurred, extends as far as the time when the sentence is uttered.

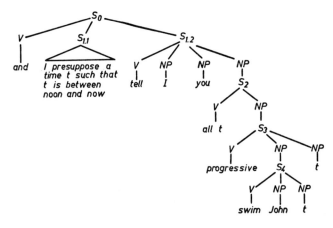

Fig. 10. Simplified deep structure of *John has been swimming*. The logical tense indication has here the form of the variable t, which is explained by the defining presupposition $S_{1.1}$. The triangle used for the presupposition denotes that its internal structure is not rendered in this tree in order to save space (for a fully rendered presupposition see fig. 16). The meaning of the tree may be expressed as follows: *I tell you that for all time t such that t is between noon and now the act of John swimming during t (has been) progressive during t.*

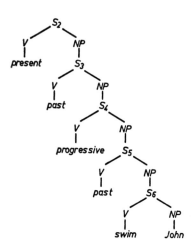

Fig. 11. Simplified intermediate structure of the S_2-dominated subtree of fig. 10 after addition of tense predicates. *Present* has here as antecedent the deleted deep structure predicate *all t.*

121

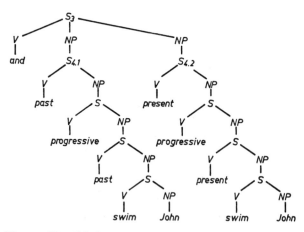

Fig. 12. Simplified coordinate intermediate subtree of *John has been swimming since noon* with the verbal process and the notion of progressiveness in the present as well as in the past.

In English the subtree dominated by $S_{4.2}$ is deleted before predicate-raising takes place (see section 4), whereas in German it is $S_{4.1}$ that is deleted, so as to give

(30) John schwimmt seit Mittag.

In Swedish deletion can apply optionally to either subtree.[9]

The time denoted by *yesterday* is not associated with the present tense in the same way as *since noon* is, and therefore only the predicate *past* is inserted at the level of intermediate structure (see fig. 7). How, then, can we account for a sentence such as example (7), which actually contains a present perfect together with *yesterday*? The explanation is that the combination of underlying tense predicates is such that it is only the auxiliary verb *may* that is associated with the present time, the temporal association of *yesterday* being restricted to the verb *do*. See fig. 13. Actually the non-finite *have* that here introduces the merely formal present perfect is redundant, for from a logical point of view it would have been sufficient to say

(31) *He may done it yesterday.

For an account of how this *have* is generated, see under 4 below.

---

[9] This description of the underlying tense of *since*-clauses is meant to be an amendment of that given by McCawley 1969b: 11.

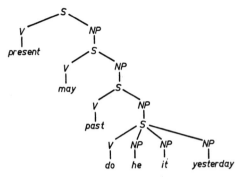

Fig. 13. Simplified intermediate subtree of *He may have done it yesterday* after insertion of tense predicates.

When the deep tense is the future, the time adverbial reduplication transformation, as stated above, inserts the tense predicate *future*. However, just as in fig. 13 the past time of *yesterday* is only associated with the principal verb *do*, not with the auxiliary verb *may*, so the future time is only associated with the principal verb, the auxiliary verb being associated with the present. Thus a simplified intermediate structure of

(32) I shall work tomorrow.

comes to have the shape shown in fig. 14 after the insertion of tense predicates. Cf. Huddleston 1969: 789.

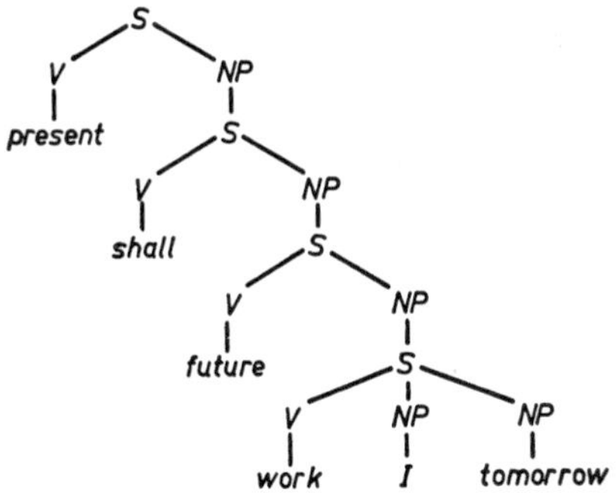

Fig. 14. Simplified intermediate subtree of *I shall work tomorrow* after insertion of tense predicates.

When, as in (24) (ii), a formal present tense in the progressive form or, as in

(33) I leave tomorrow.,

a formal simple present, denotes the future, a solution that lies near at hand is to assume that these cases are due to deletion of the auxiliary verb (cf. the term *will*-deletion in R. Lakoff 1970: 845 ff.). However, it seems preferable to assume that the present has here the same source as the historical present in English, namely that the verbal process is so vivid in the mind of the speaker that he sees it as a reality even at the time of speaking. Cf. R. Lakoff 1970: 846. Following McCawley's type of argumentation (see the above discussion about figs. 10 and 11), it is the logical existential quantifier binding the time variable that yields the tense predicate *present*, i.e. the semantic representation includes a presupposition of roughly the following content "I presuppose a time t such that t is the day that follows today" (cf. fig. 10) and a predicate of the form "exist t". This existential predicate is reduplicated by the tense predicate *present* because of the feeling the speaker has that the day of tomorrow is already present in his mind's eye. After deletion of the existential predicate, *present* becomes contiguous with the tense predicate *future*, which is associated with the futurity of the verbal action. See fig. 15.

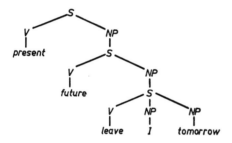

Fig. 15. Simplified intermediate subtree of *I leave tomorrow* after insertion of tense predicates and deletion of the existential quantifier which *present* refers to.

A plausible reason for the insertion of the tense predicate *present* not only in cases of this type where a formal present tense refers to the future but also in cases where *shall* and *will* are used as future tense auxiliaries (as in fig. 14) is that the future in English is always looked at from the point of view of the present. The meaning, then, of (32) can be paraphrased as "As far as can be predicted at the present moment, I shall work tomorrow" and that of (24) (ii) and (33) as "I can see in my mind's eye that I am working [I leave] tomorrow". The possibility of making these paraphrases suggests that what they express is somehow contained in the semantic representations, perhaps in the form of presuppositions of the following content "I presuppose that the future can be predicted at the present moment" in the case of (32) and "I presuppose that the future is already present in my mind's eye" in the case of (24) (ii) and (33).

The underlying tense of such sentences as (1), (18), and (19) also contains the predicate *present*, as the wish expressed applies to the time of the linguistic performance. However, a presupposition must make it clear that what is wished for has not yet been realized. See fig. 16.

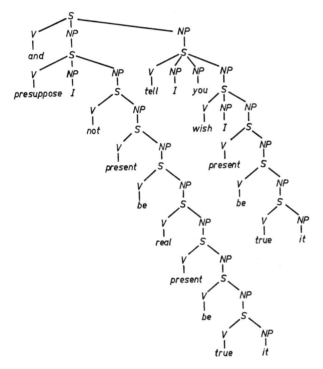

Fig. 16. Simplified intermediate structure of *I wish it was true*. The lexical item *be* has here been inserted instead of some deeper lying semantic prime or primes with the meaning *stative* or some similar meaning. The presupposition may be read as *I presuppose that it is not real that it is true*.

Inclusion of presuppositions in the semantic representations seems to be the easiest way to account for many other similar strange uses of tense, such as those described by R. Lakoff 1970: 846–48.

4. The Generation of Surface Tense

The description of tense transformations given in this section will be restricted to cases involving purely temporal and independent surface tense. This means, firstly, that I refrain from giving formalized rules how, for example, an intermediate structure such as that of fig. 16, where besides temporal relations unreality is involved, is transformed into a surface structure. An attempt to formulate rules including the participation of presuppositions in transformations has been made by Muraki (1970) in a paper on pseudo-clefting, but I am not sure how formalization on similar lines in the field of tense should be performed. Suffice it to say that the present tense underlying *is* in "*I wish it is true", which would be obtained by applying first the rules given below in (34) and then readjustment rules to fig. 16, is somehow or other transformed into a past surface tense under the influence of the unreality presupposition.

Secondly, it means that I give no rules about cases with a dependent axis. Some of these cases can probably be treated as subject to a surface constraint that turns, for example, (16) into (15) in more formal styles, in the same way as certain double negatives in the same clause are restricted to one negative in non-vulgar style. The problem of the so-called sequence of tenses in reported speech, exemplified by (15) and (16), is complicated amongst other things by the fact that dependent tense can be either deictic or non-deictic.[10] For example, (16) can only be uttered by someone who relates the adverb *tomorrow* to his own situation as well as to that of the person mentioned (i.e. "he"). Thus (15) has to be used if the next sentence is for example, "But he never turned up", as *tomorrow* is then non-deictic in relation to the one who utters (15).[11]

Another type of dependence, for which I find it hard to formulate rules, is illustrated by Mary Gallagher's example in footnote 4 above. Her conclusion is that in such cases there is no underlying tense in the main clause, so that the tense that the surface structure exhibits in this clause is simply a copy of that of the preceding relative clause.

Apart from the cases now discussed it appears possible to transform structure with intermediate tense into structure with surface tense by means of the following formula:

---

[10] Cf. Huddleston 1969: 794 (pp. 792–96 deal with reported speech).
[11] *Tomorrow* is in cases of this kind usually replaced by *on the next (following) day* but can be retained as shown by some examples in Jacobson 1964: 352–53.

(34) (i) $\begin{cases} Past + V \Rightarrow V\text{-}ed \\ Present + V \Rightarrow V\begin{Bmatrix} \text{-}s \\ \varnothing \end{Bmatrix} \end{cases}$ whenever appearing as the first two constituents of a composite predicate to which the subject–verb agreement transformation applies after predicate-raising

(ii) $\begin{cases} Past \Rightarrow have \\ Present \Rightarrow \varnothing \end{cases}$ when not the first V constituent affected by (i) above (V = predicate)

(iii) $Have$ (from $past$) $\Rightarrow \varnothing$ when preceded by another $have$ (from $past$)

(iv) $Future \Rightarrow \varnothing$

(v) $V \Rightarrow V\text{-}ed$ when preceded by $have$ (from $past$)

(vi) $V \Rightarrow V\text{-}ing$ when preceded by $progressive$

This formula implies that the following transformations take place.

(34) (i). Subject–verb agreement, which is preceded by predicate-raising, transforms certain tense predicates into bound morphemes. When applied to, for example, fig. 9, predicate-raising means that *swim* is raised into S_4, then *present swim* into S_3, and finally *progressive present swim* into S_2. Then the nodes S_3, S_4, and S_5 can be pruned so that the phrase-marker will look as in fig. 17. Here subject–verb agreement applies to the first two constituents of the composite predicate, namely *present progressive*, so that after the lexical item *be* has been inserted for *progressive* the form *be-s* is obtained. This form is later readjusted to give *is*.

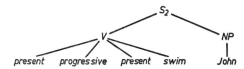

Fig. 17. The subtree of fig. 9 after predicate-raising.

Similarly, when predicate-raising is applied to fig. 7, *swim* is raised into S_2, giving *past swim*. This predicate comprises only two constituents, but, as the only ones, these constituents are also the first two, and accordingly the subject-verb agreement transformation applies, so that the form *swim-ed*, later readjusted to *swam*, is obtained.

(34) (ii). The lexical item *have* is inserted for *past*, when *past* does not appear as the first constituent of a composite V after predicate-raising, and under similar circumstances *present* is deleted. This applies, for example, to fig. 11, where *past* in S_3 is changed into *have*. This *past* first takes part in the subject–verb agreement transformation, which according to (34) (i) gives

past-s; then this form is changed by (34) (ii) into *have-s*, which is later readjusted into *has*. Similarly, in the underlying structure of such a sentence as

(35) He had been swimming.,

past past becomes first *past-ed*, then *have-ed*, and finally *had*. Fig. 9 exemplifies the deletion of *present*, when it is not the first V affected by the subject–verb agreement transformation. In this figure the instance of *present* appearing between *progressive* and *swim* is deleted after predicate-raising has taken place.

(34) (iii). If two or more instances of *have*, derived from *past*, co-occur as constituents of the same V after predicate-raising has taken place, then all but the first one are deleted. This applies, for example, to fig. 11, where the *have* derived from the second *past* is deleted.

(34) (iv). *Future* is deleted wherever it appears, as in, for example, fig. 14.

(34) (v) and (vi). A complementizer addition transformation adds *ed* to a V preceded by *have* (from *past*) and *ing* to a V preceded by *progressive*. Thus *ed* is added to *do* in fig. 13 and this *do-ed* is later readjusted into *done*. Similarly, *ing* is added to *swim* in fig. 11 after *ed* has been added to *progressive*. When later *be* replaces *progressive*, we thus get *be-ed swim-ing*, which is then readjusted into *been swimming*.

Rules (34) (ii–vi) are applied also in cases where no subject–verb agreement transformation takes place and instead transformation to infinitives, participles, or gerundive nominals (e.g. *John's having sung*, see Thomas 1966: 111 –12) occurs. Thus the present participle *having done* in (6) (ii) can be paraphrased as

(36) When he had done the job …,

and thus has a deep structure resembling that of this temporal clause, which in its derivation has two instances of the tense predicate *past*. Since in the case of participles no agreement transformation takes place, both the instances of *past* are changed into *have* by (34) (ii), after which the second of them is deleted by (34) (iii) and the first is given the ending *ing*.

However, if the sentence

(37) John's arrival caused a lot of trouble.

has the reading "The fact that John had arrived caused a lot of trouble" (cf. (8)), it is obvious that both the instances of *past* that underlie the action nominal *arrival* have been deleted. A similar case of total tense predicate deletion occurs in the derivation of possessives such as *John's*, *of England*, or *my* from underlying tensed sentences with possessive verbs.[12] Like *arrival* in (8) and (37) such possessive constructions can have several different readings according as the underlying tense varies. For example, in the sentence

(38) John's boat is new.,

it has an underlying *present*, as it can be paraphrased as "The boat that belongs to John", whereas in

(39) John's boat was wrecked by the new owner.,

it must be derived from an underlying structure with two instances of *past*, for it means "The boat that had belonged to John."

These cases of total tense predicate deletion must be accounted for by expanding the formula (34) so as to incorporate a rule of the following form

(40) Any combination of tense predicates $\Rightarrow \varnothing$ in the case of
$$\begin{cases} (a) \text{ transformation into} \\ \quad \text{action nominal} \\ (b) \text{ deletion of verb denoting} \\ \quad \text{possession} \end{cases}$$

It is worth noting that such surface structures as *John's arrival* and *John's boat* can be disambiguated to some extent by the addition of a time-relational adverb or adjective, e.g.

---

[12] Inger Ruin, in an interesting thesis, in which she successfully uses a corpus to test a theory, says (Ruin 1970: 47 ff.) that in her corpus she has several examples with a "time-free axis of orientation" for the present perfect tense. However, in "Mr Bernstead started with the air of one who has remembered important and urgent business", which is one of the examples she cites to support this view, the *of*-construction can be paraphrased as "that a person has who ...", which shows that it can be derived from an underlying structure with a possessive verb. The tense of the paraphrase verb, which also reflects the underlying tense of the *of*-construction, is here the present. I claim that it is on this underlying present tense that the present perfect tense of the *who*-clause depends. As according to this view the present perfect tense here denotes temporal precedence in relation to another tense, its axis cannot be described as "time-free"; in my opinion it is best described as non-deictic and dependent (cf. 2.2 above). The axis of the underlying present tense, on the other hand, would be non-deictic and independent, like that in (17).

A similar underlying non-deictic and independent present tense can be traced in such combinations of present perfect and future as

People who have eaten this poison will usually die in a few hours.

Here a present-tense string such as "are subject to the fate that they" can be inserted after the relative clause.

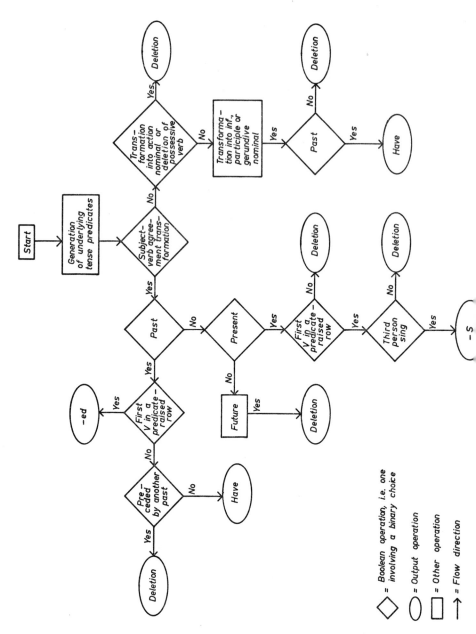

Fig. 18. Flow chart of the derivational history of underlying tense (Complementizer addition omitted).

(41) (i) John's arrival earlier in the week.

(ii) John's earlier boat (as opposed to his present boat).

This, in fact, shows the interaction of two types of tense: when formal tense fails, logical tense signalled by a time-relational expression fills its place (cf. 2.1).

The operations of the two formulas (34) and (40), on which discussion in this section has centred, have been given diagrammatic form in the flow chart depicted in fig. 18. It shows the derivational history of underlying tense predicates according to these formulas, except that for the sake of concentration the effects of complementizer addition have been omitted.

Conclusion

It has been one of the purposes of this paper to show that a full description of tense needs to take into account the five categories Logical, Formal, Deep, Intermediate, and Surface Tense. Each of them emphasizes one particular aspect of what Tense as an abstract grammatical concept really is.

The main ideas propounded in this paper may be summarized as follows:

(1) Logical tense and deep tense can be regarded as "janus" categories, i.e. synonymous categories which are looked at from different viewpoints.

(2) On the basis of deep tense intermediate tense in the form of tense predicates is generated by a special reduplication transformation.

(3) Surface tense, which is the final outcome of the derivational history of intermediate tense, and formal tense can also be regarded as "janus" categories.

The essential conclusion that can be drawn from this summary is that intermediate tense may be said to perform the function of a link that explains the relationship between the two pairs of "janus" categories logical tense/ deep tense and surface tense/formal tense. See fig. 19.

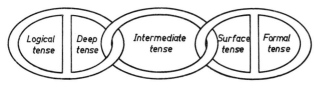

Fig. 19. Intermediate tense as a link in a chain joining the double-links logical tense/deep tense and surface tense/formal tense.

Key to Symbols and Abbreviations

Symbols

→	PS rule arrow = 'is to be rewritten as'
⇒	T rule arrow = 'is transformed into'
⟨ ⟩	angle brackets enclose node admissibility conditions
( )	round brackets in PS rules enclose optional constituents
[ ]	square brackets enclose (a) features and their realizations as words or morphemes in the terminal string, (b) constituents which are dominated by a preceding lowered constituent. For example, $_{Aux}[+tn, be]$ means that Aux dominates $[+tn]$ and *be*. For a slightly different notation see fig. 4*b* in paper no. 7.
{ }	braces in PS rules and T rules enclose alternatives
⩾	'is at least'
+	plus-sign = (a) positive value of binary feature, (b) category boundary or morphemic adherence
−	minus-sign = negative value of binary feature
△	(a) a small triangle in a terminal string = dummy symbol, (b) a large triangle in a phrase-marker configuration = constituent not analysed in detail
Ø	zero
⌢	(a) in paper no. 5 = morphemic adherence, (b) in paper no. 7 = category boundary
#	double cross = sentence boundary ringed double cross = intonation morpheme indicating where surface structure sentences end
*	asterisk = ungrammatical, or unacceptable, expression
:	colon in references (from paper no. 4 onwards), e.g. Chomsky 1965: 7, = page/s)

Abbreviations

a	referential index constant (see paper no. 7, section 1 b)
Adj	adjective
Adv_a	attributive adverbial
Adv	adverb
Advl	adverbial
AdvP	adverb phrase
ag	agent
AgP	agent phrase
Aux	auxiliary
b, b_1	referential index constants (see paper no. 7, section 1 b)
BSP	Anne Bernays. 1964. *Short Pleasures*. Pocket Books 7022.
c, c_1, c_3	referential index constants (see paper no. 7, section 1 b)
Conj	conjunction
Coord	coordinator
Cop	copula
CS rules	(a) constituent structure

	rules, (b) context sensitive rules (paper no. 1, fn. 5)	par.	paragraph
C-terminal	constituent-terminal	Part	particle
D	determiner	Pass	passive
d₁	constant (see paper no. 7, section 1 b)	Perf	perfect
		plur	plural
		P-marker	phrase-marker
def	definite	Post-T	post-transformational, i.e. after the particular transformation described
Dem	demonstrative		
ed.	edition, edited, editor		
eds.	editors	pp.	pages
emph	emphasis	Pr	predicative
GLG	Gleason 1965	Pred	predicative
ff.	'and the pages that follow'	Pres	present
fn.	footnote	Pre-T	pre-transformational, i.e. before the particular transformation described
HAI	William T. Hagan. 1961. *American Indians*. Chicago: The University of Chicago Press.		
		Prev	preverb
		PRO	vague, indefinite category, e.g. *some*, *thing*, or category substituting for another category, e.g. *it*.
HWC	Herman Wouk. 1961. *The Caine Mutiny*. New York: Doubleday.		
I	imperative morpheme	pro	feature denoting the above
IC	immediate constituent	prog	progressive
JHA	James Leo Herlihy. 1962. *All Fall Down*. Penguin Books 1742.	Prt	particle
		PS	phrase structure
		Q	question morpheme
JUR	John Updike. 1962. *Rabbit, Run*. Crest Books R 538.	S	(a) sentence, (b) subject (in paper no. 4, section 2)
Loc	locative	Seq	sequence sentence
M	modal auxiliary	sing	singular
M1, M2, etc.	subdivisions of mid-position	SVO	subject–verb–object
		T	(a) transformation, transformational, (b) anticipatory *there* (in paper no. 4, section 2)
Man	manner adverbial		
Mph	morpheme		
MV	main verb		
N	noun	Tm	time
n.	note	Tn	tense
neg	negative	TSO	*The Sunday Oregonian*. January 29, 1967.
NID₃	*Webster's Third New International Dictionary*		
		TVR	TV-recordings made by the author in the USA in 1965.
Nom	nominal	V	verb
Nom mph	nominalization morpheme	VB	verbal
NP	noun phrase	Vᵢ	intransitive verb
P	main verb or copula complement	VP	verb phrase
p.	page	VSO	verb–subject–object

133

V_t transitive verb

W string variable (see paper no. 5, section 2)

WOM William H. Whyte. 1963. *The Organization Man.* Pelican Books A 538.

X string variable (see paper no. 5, section 2)

x variable (see paper no. 7, section 1)

$X_1, X_2,$ etc. terms involved in a transformation

Y string variable (see paper no. 5, section 2)

y referential index variable (see paper no. 7 section 1 b)

Z string variable (see paper no. 5, section 2)

z referential index variable (see paper no. 7, section 1 b)

Bibliography

Bach, Emmon, 1964. *An Introduction to Transformational Grammars.* New York: Holt, Rinehart and Winston.

—— 1967. "*Have* and *be* in English syntax." *Language* 43: 462–85.

Binnick, Robert. 1969. "An application of an Extended Generative Semantic Model of Language to Man-machine Interaction." Preprint no. 18 for the International Conference on Computational Linguistics. Stockholm: Research Group for Quantitative Linguistics.

Binnick, Robert, Green, Georgia and Morgan, Jerry. 1968. *Camelot, 1968.* University of Chicago, mimeo.

Bull, W. E. 1960. *Time, Tense and the Verb.* Berkeley and Los Angeles: University of California Press.

Carlehäll, Olle. 1966. *Tense and Mood in Conditional Constructions Containing an* if-*Clause in Present-day British Prose.* Unpublished Fil. lic. thesis. Uppsala University, English Department.

Chomsky, Noam. 1957. *Syntactic Structures.* The Hague: Mouton. (The second printing, 1962, contains additional bibliography.)

—— 1959. "On Certain Formal Properties of Grammars." *Information and Control* 2: 137–67.

—— 1961. "On the Notion 'Rule of Grammar'." In *Structure of Language and its Mathematical Aspects* (identical with *Proceedings of Symposia in Applied Mathematics,* Vol. XII), pp. 6–24. Ed. by Roman Jakobson. Providence: American Mathematical Society. (Symposium held in New York City in 1960.)

—— 1964a. "The Logical Basis of Linguistic Theory." In *Proceedings of the IX International Congress of Linguists,* pp. 914–78. The Hague: Mouton. (Congress held in Cambridge, Mass., in 1962.)

—— 1964b. *Current Issues in Linguistic Theory.* The Hague: Mouton. (A revised and expanded version of Chomsky 1964a.)

—— 1965. *Aspects of the Theory of Syntax.* Cambridge, Mass.: M.I.T. Press.

—— 1967. "Remarks on Nominalization." Mimeo by the Linguistics Club, Indiana University. To appear in R. Jacobs and P. S. Rosenbaum, eds., *Readings in English Transformational Grammar.* New York: Blaisdell.

—— 1968. "Deep Structure, Surface Structure, and Semantic Interpretation." Mimeo by the Linguistics Club, Indiana University. To appear in L. Jakobovits and D. Steinberg, eds., *Semantics: An Interdisciplinary Reader;* Urbana, Ill.: University of Illinois Press.

Chomsky, Noam, and Halle, Morris. 1968. *The Sound Pattern of English.* New York: Harper & Row.

Curme, George O. 1931. *Syntax.* Boston, Mass.: Heath and Company.

Dallaire. 1963. Panel member in a discussion on "The Transformation Theory: Advantages and Disadvantages". *Report of the 13th Annual Round Table Meeting on Linguistics and Language Studies* (= *Monograph Series on Language and Linguistics, No. 15*), pp. 3–50. Washington D.C.: Georgetown University Press.

Ellegård, Alvar (in preparation). *Svensk-engelsk transformationsgrammatik.* Preliminary offset edition published in 1969. Lund: Gleerups.

Elson, Benjamin and Pickett, Velma. 1965. *An Introduction to Morphology and Syntax.* Santa Ana, Calif.: Summer Institute of Linguistics.

Fillmore, Charles J. 1963. "The Position of Embedding Transformations in a Grammar." *Word* 19: 208–31.

—— 1966. "A Proposal Concerning English Prepositions." *Georgetown University Monographs on Languages and Linguistics* 19: 19–34.

—— 1968. "The Case for Case." In *Universals in Linguistic Theory*, pp. 1–88. Ed. by Emmon Bach and Robert T. Harms. New York: Holt, Rinehart and Winston.

Gabrielson, Arvid. 1950. *Engelsk grammatik för universitet och högskolor.* 2nd ed. Stockholm: Bonniers.

Gallagher, Mary. 1970. "Adverbs of Time and Tense." In *Papers from the Sixth Regional Meeting, Chicago Linguistic Society*, pp. 220–25. Chicago, Ill.: Chicago Linguistic Society.

Gleason, H. A., Jr. 1961. *An Introduction to Descriptive Linguistics*, rev. ed. New York: Holt, Rinehart and Winston.

—— 1965. *Linguistics and English Grammar.* New York: Holt, Rinehart and Winston.

Grady, Michael. 1967. "On the Essential Nominalizing Function of English *-ing.*" *Linguistics* 34: 5–11.

Greenbaum, Sidney. 1969. *Studies in English Adverbial Usage.* London: Longmans.

Hallander, Lars-G. 1966. *Old English Verbs in -sian. A Semantic and Derivational Study.* Stockholm: Almqvist & Wiksell.

Halliday, M. A. K. 1961. "Categories of the Theory of Grammar." *Word* 17: 241–92.

Huddleston, Rodney. 1969. "Some observations on tense and deixis in English." *Language* 45: 777–806.

Jackendoff, R. 1968. "An Interpretive Theory of Pronouns and Reflexives." Mimeo by the Linguistics Club, Indiana University.

Jacobs, Roderick A. and Rosenbaum, Peter S. 1968. *English Transformational Grammar.* Waltham, Mass.: Blaisdell.

Jacobson, Sven. 1964. *Adverbial Positions in English.* Stockholm: AB Studentbok.

—— 1966. Review of Chomsky 1965. *Linguistics* 28: 111–126.

—— 1967. "Transformational Grammar and Linguistic Intuition." *Studies in Modern Philology*, New Series 3, pp. 111–14. Stockholm: Almqvist & Wiksell.

—— 1968a. "The Problem of Describing Syntactic Complexity." Special number of *Studia Neophilologica* in honour of Professor Erik Tengstrand, pp. 114–29.

—— 1968 *b*. Review of Rydén 1966. *Linguistics* 45: 118–27.

—— 1970. "An Example of the Positioning of Concurrent Adverbs." *Moderna Språk* 64: 139–47.

—— (in preparation). *On the Generation, Classification, and Positioning of Preverbs*. To be published in the series *Stockholm Studies in English*.

Jespersen, Otto. 1933. *Essentials of English Grammar*. London: George Allen & Unwin.

Katz, Jerrold J. 1970. "Interpretative Semantics vs. Generative Semantics." *Foundations of Language* 6: 220–59.

Katz, Jerrold J. and Fodor, Jerry A. 1963. "The Structure of a Semantic Theory." *Language* 39: 170–210.

Katz, Jerrold J. and Postal, Paul M. 1964. *An Integrated Theory of Linguistic Descriptions*. Cambridge, Mass.: M.I.T. Press.

Keyser, S. J. 1967. Review of Jacobson 1964. Mimeo. Waltham, Mass.: Brandeis University.

—— 1968. = Keyser 1967. *Language* 44: 357–74.

Klima, Edward S. 1964. "Negation in English." In *The Structure of Language*, pp. 246–323. Ed. by Jerry A. Fodor and Jerrold J. Katz. Englewood Cliffs, N. J.: Prentice Hall.

Kruisinga, E. and Erades, P. A. 1953. *An English Grammar*, I: I, 8th ed. Groningen: P. Noordhoff N. V.

Lakoff, George. 1965. *On the Nature of Syntactic Irregularity*. Report NSF-16, Harvard University Computation Laboratory. To appear in 1970 as *Irregularity in Syntax*; New York: Holt, Rinehart and Winston.

—— 1966. "Deep and Surface Grammar." Unpublished paper. Mimeo by the Linguistics Club, Indiana University, July, 1968.

—— 1967. *Pronominalization and the Analysis of Adverbs*. Department of Linguistics and The Computation Laboratory, Harvard University, mimeo.

—— 1970. *Linguistics and Natural Logic*. Ann Arbor, Mich.: University of Michigan.

—— Forthcoming. *Generative Semantics*. New York: Holt, Rinehart and Winston.

Lakoff, Robin. 1970. "Tense and its relation to participants." *Language* 46: 838–49.

Langendoen, D. Terence. 1969. *The Study of Syntax*. New York: Holt, Rinehart and Winston.

Lees, Robert B. 1962. "The Grammatical Basis of Some Semantic Notions." *Report of the 11th Annual Round Table Meeting on Linguistics and Language Studies* (= *Monograph Series on Language and Linguistics*, No. 13), pp. 5–20. Washington D.C.: Georgetown University Press.

—— 1963. *The Grammar of English Nominalizations*. 2nd printing. The Hague: Mouton. (First published in 1960 by the Indiana University Research Center in Anthropology, Folklore, and Linguistics.)

Ljung, Magnus. 1965. "Transformational Grammar." *Moderna språk* 59: 397–411.

Lyons, John. 1968. *Introduction to Theoretical Linguistics.* London: Cambridge University Press.

—— 1970. "The meaning of meaning." *The Times Literary Supplement* 23.7.1970, pp. 795–97.

McCawley, James D. 1967. "Meaning and the Description of Languages." *Kotoba no Uchu,* Tokyo, Nos. 9 (pp. 10–18), 10 (pp. 38–48), and 11 (pp. 51–57).

—— 1968 a. "Concerning the Base Component of a Transformational Grammar." *Foundations of Language* 4: 243–69.

—— 1968 b. "Lexical Insertion in a Transformational Grammar without Deep Structure." In *Papers from the Fourth Regional Meeting, Chicago Linguistic Society,* pp. 71–80. Ed. by B. Darden, C.-J. N. Bailey, and A. Davison. Chicago, Ill.: Department of Linguistics, University of Chicago.

—— 1969 a. "Where do Noun Phrases Come from?" Rev. ed. University of Chicago, mimeo. To appear in R. Jacobs and P. S. Rosenbaum, eds., *Readings in English Transformational Grammar*; New York: Blaisdell.

—— 1969 b. "Tense and Time Reference in English." University of Chicago, mimeo. To appear in Charles J. Fillmore and D. Terence Langendoen, eds., *Proceedings of the First Ohio State Conference on Semantics*; Chicago: Linguistics Department, University of Chicago.

—— 1969 c. "Semantic Representation." Paper prepared for the symposium on Cognitive Studies and Artificial Intelligence Research at the University of Chicago. To appear in Paul Garvin, ed., *Cognition: A Multiple View*; New York: Spartan Books.

—— 1970. "English as a VSO Language." *Language* 46: 286–99.

Muraki, Masa. 1970. "Presupposition and Pseudo-clefting." In *Papers from the Sixth Regional Meeting, Chicago Linguistic Society,* pp. 390–99. Chicago, Ill.: Chicago Linguistic Society.

Newmeyer, Frederick J. 1970. "On the Alleged Boundary between Syntax and Semantics." *Foundations of Language* 6: 178–86.

Perlmutter, David M. 1968. *Deep and Surface Structure Constraints in Syntax.* Unpublished M.I.T. doctoral dissertation. Mimeo by Osculd, Göteborg University (Ch. 5).

Pike, Kenneth L. 1954–60. *Language in Relation to a Unified Theory of Human Behavior,* Vols. I–III. Glendale, Calif.: Summer Institute of Linguistics.

Postal, Paul M. 1964. *Constituent Structure.* The Hague: Mouton.

Ross, John Robert. 1967 a. *Constraints on Variables in Syntax.* Ph.D. diss., M.I.T. Mimeo by the Linguistics Club, Indiana University.

—— 1967 b. "Auxiliaries as Main Verbs." M.I.T., mimeo. Published in 1969 in *Studies in Philosophical Linguistics,* Series 1, pp. 77–102. Ed. by William Todd. Evanston, Ill.: Great Expectations.

—— 1968. "On Declarative Sentences." M.I.T., mimeo. To appear in R. Jacobs and P. S. Rosenbaum, eds., *Readings in English Transformational Grammar*; New York: Blaisdell.

Ruin, Inger. 1970. *A Study of the Function of the Present Perfect Tense in the English Tense System*. Ph.D. diss. Mimeo. Stockholm: Stockholm University.

Rydén, Mats. 1966. *Relative Constructions in Early Sixteenth Century English*. Uppsala: Almqvist & Wiksell.

Schachter, Paul. 1964. "Kernel and Non-Kernel Sentences in Transformational Grammar." In *Proceedings of the IX International Congress of Linguists*, pp. 692–96. The Hague: Mouton. (Congress held in Cambridge, Mass., in 1962.)

Staal, J. F. 1968. "And." *Journal of Linguistics* 4: 79–81.

Stockwell, Robert P. 1960. "The Place of Intonation in a Generative Grammar of English." *Language* 36: 360–67.

—— 1964. Review of Barbara Strang, *Modern English Structure* (London, Arnold, 1962). *Language* 40: 483–87.

Svartvik, Jan. 1966. *On Voice in the English Verb*. The Hague: Mouton.

—— 1967. "A New Generation of Passives." Göteborg University, mimeo. Published in 1970 in *Actes du Xe Congrès International des Linguistes*, pp. 1137–44. Bucharest : L'Académie de la République Socialiste de Roumanie. (Congress held in Bucharest in 1967.)

Thomas, Owen. 1966. *Transformational Grammar and the Teacher of English*. New York: Holt, Rinehart and Winston.

Webster's Third New International Dictionary. 1964. Springfield, Mass.: G. & C. Merriam Company.

Wyld, H. C. 1952. *The Universal Dictionary of the English Language*. London: Routledge & Kegan Paul.